THE GET TO THE POINT! GUIDE TO BEATING DEPRESSION

GET TO THE POINT—AND GET OUT OF YOUR RUT!

Depression affects millions of people every day—but help is at hand. *The Get to the Point! Guide to Beating Depression* provides a wide range of simple, easy-to-implement solutions proven to alleviate the symptoms of depression and fight its root causes, safely and effectively. Between these covers you will find effective tips and tricks to control depression and halt its progression along with up to the minute information detailing the very latest cutting-edge advances in medical science, new and exciting solutions for treatment-resistant depression, and advice on staying depression-free for life.

Don't suffer one minute longer than necessary— start reading *The Get to the Point! Guide to Beating Depression* now and get back to living your life today.

THE GET TO THE POINT! GUIDE TO BEATING DEPRESSION

MARC ALLAN MOORE

CONTENTS

INTRODUCTION

No matter one's position in life, little is more effective at keeping a human being from the enjoyment of life than depression. When in the throes of a depressive spell, everyday activities can seem impossible to handle, and difficult situations may well appear insurmountable. Worse, depression's ability to cloud objectivity and judgment can be frighteningly potent, effectively deepening the conditions which may have led to its onset in the first place and maintaining the state of depression as an ongoing situation. Many individuals suffering from depression are unable to visualize any route back to normalcy, allowing the roots of depression to become so deeply embedded in their lives that they begin to see it as part of their normal state—and at that point, even imagining a life without depression can become next to impossible.

Fortunately, many solutions to the problems brought on by depression exist. Even better, several of these solutions can be implemented without incurring additional financial expense or adding to the depression sufferer's already weighty psychological burden. Depending on the severity of your depression, relief from your depressive symptoms may be as close as a few minutes away—and even more serious cases can often be mitigated without the need for psychoactive medication or more invasive treatment.

Unfortunately, popular portrayals of depression as shown in movies, television and other media have led to widespread misunderstandings about depression becoming commonplace, as well as some outright falsehoods. Depressed people are frequently depicted as simply 'sad' or easily fixed solely for the purposes of convenience of storytelling. While this in itself is not necessarily harmful—after all, it is rarely the purpose of entertainment to provide medically accurate information—these overly simplistic depictions encourage simple, direct solutions which may not work in real life, or which may function as only one part of a multi-pronged treatment for depression.

As a result, many people suffering from depression are often reluctant to seek help, believing they are not suffering from severe enough symptoms to justify taking corrective action, or doubting that treatment will help them based on their limited understanding of its effectiveness. Others resist addressing their depression out of denial, thinking themselves able to 'tough it out' or 'push through' on their own, perhaps after a lifetime of having been administered similar advice by well-meaning family and friends. But lacking a solid and evidence-based plan of action, most tend to fall back into depression sooner or later as a result of having failed to properly address the underlying causes of their condition, nor the environmental stresses, unhealthy patterns, inadequate nutrition, and many other factors which can contribute to depression.

In times past, a diagnosis of depression could bear social stigma that many were justifiably leery to have applied to themselves, but it should be emphasized that depression is absolutely nothing to be ashamed of. And perhaps even more importantly, neither is seeking treatment for one's depression. Quite the contrary, those who are able to take the necessary steps forward to correct issues which may have bedeviled their entire lives should be applauded for their courage, not derided—for far from a mere symptom of weakness or an imaginary ailment, depression is a widely recognized, serious condition that has been established time and again both through clinical research and scientific studies, and which has long-term debilitating effects if left unaddressed.

You may have tried and failed to beat your depression in the past, possibly multiple times; and perhaps, these failed efforts have continued to haunt and hinder you ever since. If so, rest assured that while these attempts may not have previously succeeded at mitigating your problems, they still represent steps in the right direction and you should view them as such. In some cases, these past experiences may lead you away from trying certain methods suggested within these pages, yet while we are beginning our journey I would encourage you to maintain an open mindset even towards methods of depression management which may not have seemed to succeed for you in the past. As we'll quickly see, most successful plans to reduce or eliminate depression depend on multi-pronged strategies—so when you pin all your hopes on one specific approach, particularly in the depths of an acute depression, it's all too easy to prematurely conclude that method has failed. In truth, had that strategy been used as part of a more comprehensive program to address and reduce your depressive symptoms, it is completely possible that it might well eventually have succeeded, at least in part.

Ultimately, no single one of these strategies may suffice to manage your depression—but by trying and combining multiple methods, eventually you should be able to discover enough management tools to let you control your depression and live your life without fear, knowing that when the prospect of depression rears its ugly head once more, you'll be fully confident in your ability to rein it in without letting yourself get dragged back to square one.

No matter how you feel at this moment, take heart: you should be congratulated for setting forth on this journey to navigate your way out of the maze of depression. This voyage may not be a short one, it may not be entirely pleasant, and it may be more work than expected, yet I can promise you with complete certainty that it is absolutely worth every effort you can bring to it. Remember this above all else: when it comes to fighting depression, there is no such thing as wasted effort. Although sometimes it may not feel that way when you're fighting an uphill battle, each step you take, no matter how seemingly small, brings you that much closer to your goal of living your life without suffering the effects of depression. And isn't that worth it, no matter the cost?

CHAPTER 1

WHAT IS DEPRESSION?

ANY BASIC DEFINITION of depression essentially describes the condition as a mood disorder characterized by unshakable sadness or inability to engage with life. However, as any sufferer of depression will tell you, such brief descriptions can be deceptively minimizing.

From a medical perspective, the definition of depression is laid out in the *Diagnostic and Statistical Manual of Mental Disorders, Fifth Edition*, the most recent update (as of this writing) of the American Psychiatric Association's encyclopedic text classifying and elaborating upon the range of commonly seen conditions affecting the mind. Basically, a clinical diagnosis of depression depends upon the following nine symptoms:

- Suffering from a depressed mood, characterized by feelings of sadness, emptiness, hopelessness, or irritability, the latter particularly in children and adolescents

- Significantly diminished interest or inability to take pleasure in regular activities
- Significant weight loss or weight gain totaling more than five percent of one's body weight in a single month or marked decrease or increase in appetite
- Insomnia, defined as the inability to fall asleep or to remain asleep, or hypersomnia, defined as excessive daytime sleepiness, sleeping more than ten hours each day, or inability to feel refreshed after sleeping
- Psychomotor agitation, defined as purposeless actions such as wringing of hands, pacing, finger-tapping and other such repetitive motions; or psychomotor retardation, defined as a visible slowing of physical movement or speech
- Chronic fatigue or loss of energy
- Continual feelings of worthlessness or excessive or inappropriate guilt
- Significantly diminished ability to think or concentrate regularly, or chronic indecisiveness
- Recurrent thoughts of death or suicide which can surface at any time, seemingly without cause

For the purposes of this book, we will not concern ourselves too much with the strict clinical boundaries of depression, nor restrict our advice to those who have previously obtained a diagnosis of depression from a psychiatrist, physician, or other medical professional. Technically, the symptoms above are intended to describe what is referred to as Major Depressive Disorder, for which a patient should display five or more of the above symptoms, including one or both of the first two, occurring during much of the day, nearly every day, during a two-week period. However, if you feel excluded by the strict limitations implied therein, don't worry. I myself avoided seeking help or gaining additional coping skills to deal with my own depressive tendencies for years, feeling my own problems didn't necessarily rise to the level of a 'major' depressive issue and therefore fell outside the range of what medical professionals were inclined to treat. If you feel you suffer from depression enough that you can recognize patterns of your own behavior within the above definition, it shouldn't stop you from seeking help if you only exhibit four of nine symptoms or you don't feel that way every day for fourteen days— anything you can do to reduce your emotional burden is worthwhile, even if you may not strictly fit the above clinical definition.

As you can see, depression can manifest in a number of seemingly contradictory ways. Symptoms can be defined as both too much or too little of a range of factors, including sleep, activity, mood, motivation, and weight—and exactly what constitutes 'too much' or 'too little' can be a subjective decision, either on the part of the person suffering from depression or those around them. In addition, if a person's depression has been a part of their life for an extended period of time, it can be difficult for either that person or their loved ones to identify any of these factors as symptomatic of a depressive condition, instead of simply part of their personality or character.

Further, depression itself often seems to work to maintain its hold on people by undermining their confidence—even to the extent that they may become unconfident that depression is the cause of their suffering. Granted, a number of factors may combine to create the fog in which depression can mire a person, including financial troubles, lack of social connections, poor health and others, but we inevitably find that when the problems caused by depression are properly addressed, other issues become significantly easier to deal with.

Unfortunately, a large part of what can make depression so difficult to both live with and to mitigate is the nebulous, shifting nature of the condition. Simply 'fixing' one effect caused by depression is no guarantee that it won't manifest in another previously unseen range of symptoms; without addressing the underlying cause or causes, a depression sufferer may simply be exchanging one set of burdens for another. And as we have seen, depression is much harder to diagnose definitively than most medical conditions—there is no simple test to determine whether or not a patient suffers from depression.

Ultimately, the most important factor is how you feel. If you feel that alleviating the occurrence of any of the traditional symptoms of depression would improve your life, chances are good you will benefit by attempting to do so. Frankly, the negative effects of depression can be so debilitating, if you believe you suffer from depression to any degree, no matter how small, it is worth making the effort to reduce or eliminate its influence on your life. By doing so, you will almost certainly find yourself the better for the effort, and you make yourself better prepared for the future by learning skills and techniques for recognizing depressive tendencies and rooting them out before they can take hold of your psyche.

CHAPTER 2

WHAT ARE THE EFFECTS OF DEPRESSION?

AS BEFITS A CONDITION that can arise from any number of factors and manifest in a wide range of varying symptoms, depression affects each person it touches in a slightly different manner. And because depression afflicts each person differently, typical one-size-fit-all treatments are often difficult, if not impossible, to apply. One depression sufferer may experience life as if muffled under a black cloud or thick blanket, while another may feel completely unable to arise from bed or leave their apartment, and a third may not recognize any commonalities whatsoever between their condition and either of the preceding examples. But regardless of their differences, that doesn't change the underlying facts that depression affects each of their lives, albeit in different ways, and that each person's symptoms might possibly be alleviated by similar courses of action.

Where some depression manifests itself as a crippling inability to function even to the point of being unable to get out of bed in the morning—or evening—others are more or less able to go about their daily lives as if nothing was wrong. And yet, while from an external perspective it may be tempting to label the second form of depression less severe than the first, both individuals may feel remarkably similar emotions, particularly regarding his or her own self-image. One of the most insidious traits of depression is its ability to leach the joy out of life, so while those who seem able to go through the motions and successfully put up the front of a healthy, functional individual for the benefit of others might appear more functional to all intents and purposes, internally they may feel like a fraud, always one step away from exposure as the emotionally-controlled wreck they feel themselves to be. Conversely, the individual who is unable to leave their apartment or interact with others comfortably may feel they are mitigating their condition to the degree necessary, maintaining the stability of their internal life by managing their level of contact with the outside world and the stresses it can inflict, and might not describe him- or herself as depressed at all as a result.

What these examples demonstrate is that while it's tempting to categorize and evaluate depression's effects as if they can be ranked in terms of severity, without knowing precisely how they impact the person in question it's impossible to know how deep that impact may run. And perhaps more immediately relevant for the depression sufferer, I urge you not to judge your own symptoms of depression against what you perceive to be 'normalcy' as experienced by other individuals—for without knowing precisely how others are affected by their own emotional issues, we cannot know what burdens they might have had to overcome. In far more cases than you might realize, a wide smile can mask a darkened heart, or a blank face conceal a long, hard road both behind and ahead.

Whatever your personal relationship with depression and its symptoms, I encourage you not to feel as if your problems are either insurmountable or insignificant. To whatever degree you suffer from depression, it's an inarguable fact that your enjoyment of life will be meaningfully enhanced by addressing and treating the factors preventing you from full immersion in the reality that surrounds you.

The truth is, people react in vastly different ways to identical situations, often based upon their past experience and current emotional state. Even when situations are carefully crafted to produce specific responses, such as theme parks or movies, it's impossible to evoke identical reactions in all people—when was the last time everyone you know agreed on a film, political candidate, or even a restaurant's cuisine? And thanks to the wide and varied range of effects depression can cause, it's impossible to predict precisely how a specific depression sufferer may or may not react to a specific situation—or a treatment intended to ameliorate their symptoms.

Chances are very good that you have a certain idea of just how depression affects you. But it's just as likely that those people close to you have their own ideas—and if you could look at yourself through their eyes, you might be surprised how widely those ideas might diverge.

As described in the clinical definition provided in the previous chapter, the medical definition of Major Depressive Disorder centers around nine commonly accepted symptoms. However, the affliction of depression can manifest in a wide variety of symptoms, and regardless of the severity of your own depressive tendencies you may or may not demonstrate any of the following during a depressive episode:

- Sadness
- Fatigue and lethargy
- Insomnia
- Negative thoughts
- Mood swings
- Hypersensitivity
- Irritability
- Difficulty concentrating
- Forgetfulness
- Back pain
- Headaches
- Lack of appetite
- Gastrointestinal distress
- Withdrawal
- Inability to enjoy pleasurable activities
- Loss or decrease in libido
- Recurrent thoughts of death or suicide

Some of these symptoms may come and go seemingly at random, while others can seem to persist through a depressive person's entire waking existence. Yet what they all have in common is that they all spring from the same root cause: the sufferer's untreated depressive tendencies, as defined by their unique brain chemistry, the emotional events that have impacted upon their lives, and their other unique qualities.

Because so much of one's emotional state is controlled by internal chemistry and environmental factors over which we may have little to no control, these tendencies are often seen in multiple members of the same family, passed down from parent to child for generation after generation. In such cases, common symptoms may be seen either as a result of similar genetic background or childhood conditions, but individual family members' experiences of depression may just as likely be wildly disparate, seemingly having little in common with each other. And due to the unique lack of perspective people often tend to have when looking upon our own family, you might not even realize a close family member suffers from the same symptoms until you confront those symptoms within yourself, having always accepted those qualities of their personality affected by depression as simply part of who they are. Who among us with siblings has not found it difficult to understand why others might say you seem similar to them, when it seems so plainly obvious to you that you share little to nothing in common? In all likelihood, the truth may lie somewhere in between what is perceived by others and that which you believe to be true. Yet it is impossible to deny the effects family can have upon our psyches, both during our childhoods and lasting well into our adult lives, if not over the course of one's entire existence. For this reason, you may find it illuminating to examine your family members for clues to your own emotional state, and perhaps even share your quest for self-improvement with them—although I would caution you against placing too much attachment upon expecting your own perspectives, opinions, and experiences to be confirmed by relatives, even those to whom you might feel the closest.

By seeking treatment for your depression, in fact, you may experience surprising pushback from family members or friends. For example, you might make what you think of as an offhand comment about something you've discovered about yourself and the way depression manifests in your life, intending absolutely nothing more by it than its surface meaning, only to be greeted with either groaning denial or fierce rebuking. When we receive this type of feedback from people who play important roles in our lives such as parents, spouses, siblings, close friends, or even children, it can be disheartening, particularly if improving your relationships with those selfsame people is one of your motivating factors for self-improvement. If this happens to you, console yourself: in all likelihood, their reactions have far more to do with their own internal experience of life than with any judgment upon you, your actions, or your attempts at beating back your depressive symptoms. Unfortunately, the myriad complexities of interpersonal relationships mean that sometimes the people you would expect to be the most supportive of your efforts to get well can turn out to be those who seem most determined to stand in your way.

In many cases, family members who might have had a hand in your upbringing may tend to see any attempt at self-improvement on your part only through the lens of their own experience, taking your attempt to get better as a comment on their actions. As we've seen, the effects of depression can be insidious—and while depression is not technically a contagious disease, it is undeniable that similar strains of the affliction can run in families. Because of this, it is quite likely these people might also have been denying or attempting to ignore their own similar problems rather than face up to them—and by making the effort to do so yourself, it's possible that in their eyes, you have inadvertently highlighted their inaction.

Don't be discouraged. The only thing more difficult than

pulling yourself out of depression is trying to pull someone else out of theirs—in all likelihood, the attempt will only leave both parties hopelessly mired in emotional quicksand. In such circumstances, if you cannot convince the other person to seek treatment or to work at bettering him- or herself, your best option will most likely be to plunge ahead with your own efforts at self-improvement and hope that your success will set an example showing others in your life that change is not impossible—and that the experience of life can truly be that much sweeter once one has done the work to address and remediate the effects of depression.

CHAPTER 3

WHY DOES DEPRESSION EXIST?

AS FAMILIAR AS its symptoms may seem, the underlying root causes of depression can be difficult for many to figure out. Because the amount of suffering the condition produces often seems disproportionate to the underlying emotional events tied to its origins, it might seem that once we have adequately addressed those root causes that depression should vanish, or at least diminish to the point of becoming relatively easy to manage. Yet in many cases, the emotional impact remains or even increases well after the point when we believe we have properly come to terms with upheavals that may have occurred years or even decades prior. And for many, the question ultimately remains: why is my mind doing this to me, and to what end? After all, when we suffer a physical injury such as a cut or bruise, our body acts to heal the wound as rapidly and effectively as possible, often leaving no indication the injury ever occurred once the healing process is complete. So why doesn't the mind work similarly?

It would certainly be nice if it worked that way, but in truth, the mind is the most complicated and difficult to understand part of the human organism. As a result, our understanding of its workings and functions lags significantly behind more easily understood systems—as crucially important as the heart is to the body's functioning, we now know most of the poetic imagery placed upon it by philosophers and theorists of the past was unwarranted, and it is essentially a large, strong muscle. Conversely, the mind holds nearly all of what we think of as both personality and the underlying programming that keeps the rest of the organism functioning, both consciously and subconsciously, along with retaining memories, interpreting all number of signals from the nervous system, and performing many other vital tasks.

In truth, this dichotomy between the mind and the body is an oversimplification of a complex, symbiotic relationship; just as the mind is part of the body, the body cannot function without the mind. And by taking a more integrated viewpoint of the mind-body connection, we begin to perceive the interdependent relationships between the body's many systems as an essential balancing act—one which evolved over millions of years, the preponderance of which bore little to no resemblance to the daily existence of modern life.

The roots of the condition we know as depression lie deep in the past, in a time when life was much more focused on day-to-day survival, when it was most likely intended to function as a sort of early warning system. During an era when merely finding enough food to allow for subsistence and locating shelter were the primary problems facing a human being each day, the state of high alert signified by depression would have been an exceedingly rare occasion, as the conditions of life in those times ensured the symptoms of depression might only be experienced by any one person during a few extreme times over the course of their entire lives.

The rapid rate of change in human existence over the past few hundred years has produced a massive gulf between the day-to-day lives most humans lived for the overwhelming majority of history and the life you live today. While many advances have inarguably been positive, the simple fact is that evolution is an exceedingly slow process. As such, our bodies have not had nearly enough time to adapt to any number of modern habits such as sitting for a large portion of the day, the wide availability of calorie-rich and carbohydrate-heavy foods, and other facts of modern existence we take for granted. Because our perspectives are limited to our own existence (and perhaps those of our older relatives), few of us have any experience of the type of existence millions of years of evolution shaped and designed our bodies to cope with. Even those who endeavor to understand such conditions generally do so under limited, controlled circumstances, with the aid of enough modern conveniences to limit their suffering—and let us be frank, suffering was the primary hallmark of the hardscrabble existence lived by humanity for much of that time, lest we idealize our ancestors as some sort of noble savages living in harmony with nature in some early primitive Garden of Eden. In truth, life in those times was tougher than most of us today can hope to conceive.

Unfortunately, as the human race has progressed, depression has adjusted more quickly than our bodies are able to. Instead of becoming triggered by problems that threaten our very survival, now depressive symptoms are more often brought on by the far more common issues we encounter regularly: financial problems, emotional upheaval, or even common everyday irritations. At the same time, the changes in human lifestyle created by widespread industrialization and other byproducts of civilization have led to a massive reduction in factors that once would have held depression at bay. Along with time spent outdoors, the amount of exercise an average human gets on a daily basis has plummeted, while the level of emotional and environmental stimulae a person is subjected to each day is many times higher.

When these factors are taken into account, it's easy to lay the roots of depression bare. Indeed, given the undeniably slow progress of physical evolution, it would be surprising were modern life to be completely in sync with the conditions our bodies adapted to through the preponderance of human history. But as a result, over the last century depression has come to be seen as an endemic part of the human condition, instead of what it really is: an unavoidable byproduct of the gap between the rapidly changing conditions of modern life and our physical bodies' ability to adapt to cope with said conditions. Yes, we live more comfortable lives than most of our ancestors did—but the price we pay for that is more insidious and harder to recognize than most would have ever expected.

When viewed in this manner, the prevalence of depression as a symptom of the modern human state of existence is hardly surprising; in fact, it would be shocking if many similar such problems hadn't developed. As they become better known and more widely accepted, these incontrovertible facts should bring some small comfort to those suffering the effects of depression. Rather than fretting unproductively over their symptoms and wasting time wondering whether there is something wrong with them, people shall simply revert to the obvious, simple truth that there isn't, and that instead, the immense changes in human lifestyle over the past several thousand years have simply caught up with them. Under such circumstances, the very idea of blaming oneself seems preposterous; the force of the weight of history is too much for any one person to shoulder alone.

This isn't merely an unsupported hypothesis, either. Studies of surviving cultures maintaining older ways of life, such as the Amish, have consistently demonstrated much, much lower incidence of depression and depressive symptoms, sometimes to the point that depression is essentially unknown within these societies. Of course, even were it feasible for most, we cannot simply return to the ways of the past in an attempt to battle depression: for the most part, the primitive hunter-gatherer tribal structures that comprised human society during much of that time simply don't exist anymore, and where they do it would simply be impractical for most of us to drop everything in our lives and revert to patterns of existence that were common hundreds of years before we were born. Yet, as much as is possible, that is essentially what we must find a way to do in order to bring our lives back into harmony, and minimize the chance of inflaming these ingrown tendencies and triggering depression.

How to resolve this seeming contradiction? In many ways, this is the essential conundrum of modern life: maintaining connection with those beneficial aspects of the higher level of stimulation and interconnectivity characterizing today's society without aggravating the inbuilt defenses that can elicit depressive symptoms.

Fortunately, as we'll see, while modern human existence has inarguably produced many conditions favorable to widespread tendencies toward depression, it's not all bad. While we may not be able to return to the days when much of each day was spent in a strenuous, exhausting hunt for food, through regular exercise we can ensure we get enough physical activity to mitigate the encroaching effects of depression. We also have far greater access to information and many other resources, as well as significantly more advanced scientific knowledge—we simply have to marshal these assets to work for us rather than allowing modern life to drag us down. By doing so, we can identify those specific aspects of ancestral life that have been eliminated or minimized in modern life, analyze their level of impact upon mood and body chemistry, and do what we can either to mitigate their effects or to replace those lacking aspects with their contemporary equivalents.

Depending on the severity of your depressive symptoms, I completely understand if you might have been growing impatient with these initial chapters—after all, in the midst of a depressive episode, all we really want is relief, as quickly as possible. Assuming you didn't just skip past them, however, I think you will find that a comprehensive understanding of precisely what depression is and how it came to occupy such an imposing position in the modern psyche is central to any serious effort to battle depression. Much of the fright and tension the condition brings about is rooted in its nebulous, shadowy nature; depression strikes at us from obscurity, deriving much of its power from fear of the unknown. Once we can remove or at the very least lighten this cloak of mystery, we see that far from a dark, enigmatic terror, depression is at its heart a relatively simple biological condition that just happens to produce occasionally terrifying effects—but one that has easily comprehensible causes and can be dealt with just like any other. For that reason, I believe that whenever you feel the tendrils of depression creeping back into your mind and you consult this book again, as I intend the reader to be able to do regularly, that this understanding will help mitigate depression's power to affect you, and help you come to see it as a manageable medical condition no different than any other. Depression is not a demon, an evil cloud, a curse, or an indication that there is anything fundamentally wrong with you, even if it may occasionally feel that way, and once you understand that, you take away much of its influence over your life without even needing to fight it head on.

However, now that we have gained an understanding of what depression is and where it comes from, we are ready to rally our strength and start chipping away at the barriers depression has put up in our lives, bit by bit. In the next few chapters, we'll take a look at techniques you can use to fight depression, alleviate your depressive symptoms, and maintain a depression-free lifestyle no matter what problems may come your way.

CHAPTER 4

HOW TO FIGHT DEPRESSION

TRADITIONALLY, in the past many people were taught to rely solely on resources such as counseling with their religious leader or general medical practitioner to address emotional issues, if they were taught to address emotional issues at all. As a result of this type of upbringing, some will occasionally insist that one or another technique is the one and only viable path out of depression. While simple logic should tell us that just isn't true—a condition with many causes may have at least as many cures—the unfortunate truth is, when people proffer such opinions and these traditional avenues are seen to fail, depression sufferers are likely to experience worsening symptoms, feeling that they've already grasped at their only lifeline and have now run entirely out of options. This state of desperation can be both frustrating and dangerous, as it can exacerbate depressive tendencies and intensify the likely already fragile mental state of the depression sufferer.

If this sounds reminiscent of your own experience, worry not. Today, thanks to more common understanding of the nature of depression, even the most stubborn adherent to traditional means will likely concede that clinging to one solution to the exclusion of all others may not constitute the most productive path away from emotional turmoil for all. Although religious counseling and traditional medical treatment can work for some, where depression is concerned very little is universal. Additionally, the quality of care one may find at their local house of worship or therapist's office can vary widely—after all, as humans, we are all subject to our own issues and challenges, some of which may prevent even the most well-meaning individual from providing optimal care.

Some who have tried and failed to obtain help through these avenues will turn against them, placing blame on the institution itself rather than the particular individual who failed to properly or fully ameliorate their condition. In most cases this blame is disproportionate, and often indicates a displaced self-loathing rooted in the belief that one's own inability to control their emotions indicates weakness which should be concealed. However, the truth is that depression is a wily adversary, and we should congratulate ourselves for any attempts to overcome its symptoms, no matter the outcome.

Traditional medical avenues of treatment for depression tend to come with a greater focus on diagnosis and labeling of depressive afflictions, referring to some conditions as 'endogenous depression', 'reactive depression', 'cyclic depression', or 'clinical depression'. For the purposes of this book, we will not delve too deeply into the various labels medical professionals apply to different states, but if you have previously sought medical assistance to fight your depression you may bear this diagnosis either as a hard-won badge of your affliction or as a scarlet brand upon your soul. Whatever the case, I suggest you take these terms for what they are: shorthand used by medical professionals to broadly categorize wide ranges of depressive conditions in order to bring each patient the most appropriate care possible without requiring a fresh diagnosis each time they enter a medical office. In truth, even these categories are far from ironclad, and categorization can vary depending on both the patient's condition and state of mind, as well as the education, experience, and background of the person making the diagnosis.

Further, it's worth noting that prescription antidepressants are far from the universal cure-all they are often considered in the popular imagination. Quite the contrary: most antidepressants are only effective on around thirty percent of patients they are administered to, and some drugs have not shown results significantly higher than the placebo effect. In providing these figures, I hasten to indicate that I don't mean to dissuade anyone from seeking medical assistance in defeating their depression—in fact, antidepressants have been shown to be somewhat more effective at treating the most severe cases of major depression, including cases that have proven resistant to less drastic methods—but it's worth noting that even when you take the less-than-desirable side effects some medications can produce into account, antidepressants are far from a 'magic bullet' solution.

It's telling that in the years since antidepressant drugs were first introduced in the late nineteen-fifties, the continual spread of depression has not been reduced, slowed, or inhibited even one tiny bit. Make no mistake, these drugs absolutely have their place as a useful tool in the fight against depression, and should be considered as an option by anyone suffering from its symptoms, particularly those whose depression reaches a stage where they are unable to function or begin to consider suicide—but as we have seen, depression is a difficult opponent. As such, it behooves us to use every tool at our disposal to fight it, rather than limit ourselves to a single approach or mindset, especially one which has not proven widespread efficacy across a broad range of depressive conditions.

Some people are understandably wary of seeking assistance within their community for fear of having their problems exposed, feeling that depression is indicative of weakness or mental instability. In fact, while this worry might have been justified in times past, today knowledge of depression is more widespread—if not necessarily a true understanding of it—and as such, you may be surprised to find many people within your community are liable to react more positively than you might expect, perhaps even supportively.

Often, those of us prone to depression are inclined to get caught up in consideration of the perceived unfairness of our situations. Trapped within our own perspectives, it can seem as if we alone are subject to the tortures of depression, but we forget that the effects of depression are often invisible to the naked eye. Even when human beings cohabitate, the interior struggles one faces can go unnoticed by others— not out of lack of concern, but simply because most of us tend to be wrapped up in our own problems. Rarely are any of us actively on the lookout for signs of distress around us. Indeed, when we feel the stresses of our struggles we may even misinterpret the symptoms of others' battles as reflective of our own issues, because when one is self-consumed in the midst of a depressive spell everything around is liable to be colored by the experience.

As easy as it is to say, I recognize how difficult this advice can be to follow, but when depression threatens to take hold of your senses, you must fight as hard as you can not to wallow in your negative feelings. The sense of emotional comfort wallowing offers will always prove fleeting, leaving in its wake a sense of inevitability and hopelessness that can be exhausting to climb out of. If you, like many people prone to depression, have battled with these tendencies for much of your life, you may feel a sense of familiarity when you indulge in rumination on negative thoughts. The allure of depression can be insidious, even to those who don't personally suffer its symptoms—or perhaps, particularly so. In either circumstance, however, this period of negative rumination rarely proves helpful or productive.

More often than not, overactive thoughts constitute part of the problem, even when they may seem like part of the solution. Speaking personally, I know that as a person prone to overthinking a problem, even in the depths of depression a chunk of my mind will continue churning away unrelentingly day and night, even when I know consciously there is nothing to be done to relieve the issues bedeviling me. And thanks to the ego of personality, that part of the mind insists on its own importance, offering the false hope that it might be able to ferret out some previously unseen angle from which the cloud of emotion surrounding you might be dispelled—when in all likelihood, only a willful cessation of your compulsive thoughts is likely to lighten your burden.

If you have attempted such a flight from your own negative thought patterns before, you may be wondering how best to effect such an escape. Because such thoughts tend to rattle around in your head until something else pushes them out, often the best thing you can do is to find something productive to do, giving yourself both something else to think about and to occupy the time that would otherwise be spent in rumination. If you can find a diversion that is itself a depression-fighting activity, all the better.

With that in mind, let's take a look at some proven strategies for fighting depression that you can integrate into your life and begin accelerating your road to recovery right away.

CHAPTER 5

FIGHTING DEPRESSION WITH EXERCISE

THE SINGLE MOST IMPORTANT step you can take to beat your depression is to start exercising right now. That doesn't necessarily mean to get a gym membership, sign up for a workout class, or retain the services of a personal trainer; although any or all of those options might prove to be good choices depending on how well they fit into your lifestyle, defeating depression through exercise can begin with smaller steps—literally.

When many people who tend toward a sedentary lifestyle think about exercise, they may picture large, sweaty men furiously pumping iron while lithe women perform aerobic dances, or they may have painful flashbacks to humiliations suffered in the gym classes of their adolescence. However, in reality exercise can be as simple as walking—and still be surprisingly effective at reducing the effects of depression.

With the recent popularity of fitness-tracking devices such as Fitbit and Apple Watch, along with widespread aware-ness of recent studies showing the harmful effects of constant sitting, more and more people have become aware of the importance of walking regularly. While such devices tend to emphasize the importance of walking as much as ten thousand steps a day, studies of the effects of exercise on depression have shown significant success in reducing symptoms of depression from as little as two hundred minutes of walking per week—as little as thirty minutes a day. Perhaps even more surprising, the reduction in depression symptoms from such mild, low-impact activity was essentially the same as that demonstrated by some of the most widely used antidepressant drugs. That's right: by simply incorporating a short walk or two into one's daily routine, most depression sufferers can significantly reduce their symptoms to the same degree of benefit as many prescription antidepressants, without any of the negative side effects.

Of course, it should be noted that these studies also indicate that in general, more exercise was linked to greater benefit in fighting the effects of depression. And because everyone's body is different, some individuals will inevitably require greater levels of activity than others to enjoy the same reduced level of depression symptoms. But ultimately, the conclusions of each of these studies boil down to one absolute truism: when it comes to fighting depression through exercise, virtually any level of activity is better than none, no matter how small. If you feel achieving thirty minutes of walking a day seems unachievably out of reach, then start smaller: close this book, get up now, and walk around your house, building, or apartment for five minutes, ten minutes, or as long as you feel you can comfortably stand. Then, when you feel you have recovered from your first burst of activity, try it again. Eventually, you will build up to the point where you can easily achieve thirty minutes of walking spread throughout the day, followed by being able to walk thirty minutes consecutively—but even if you don't, after only a short time you will still see some reduction in your depressive symptoms. It really is that simple: where exercise is concerned, do what you can and don't berate yourself for not being able to do more than you can reasonably achieve.

Why does exercise work so well at fighting depression? There are many theories, but primary among them is that regular exercise increases the activity of endorphins—natural chemicals produced by the body which lower awareness of pain and work to build up immunity against disease. Exercise can also help by releasing norepinephrine, a neurotransmitter that can work to improve mood directly. In addition, exercise can produce a number of long-term benefits which decrease the odds of developing deepening depressive symptoms later in life, including reduced chances of developing many types of cancer and heart disease, lowering blood pressure, and improving one's overall self-image.

There are few negatives associated with exercise as used to fight depression, but the most prominent is simply a question of opposing forces: namely, when in the depths of a depression it can be difficult to find motivation for much of anything, let alone for physical activity that may not seem necessary or directly relevant to the battle in which one is currently embroiled. However, this is primarily a problem of perception. As shown above, study after study has demonstrated a direct connection between physical activity and lowering of depressive symptoms, as well as an equal correlation between the more sedentary lifestyle that has arisen in modern times and the widespread prevalence of depression. You must keep in mind that in many ways, lack of activity *is* depression and vice versa; depressive symptoms can be interpreted as your body's signal that you need to get up and move it more often, for your own good both physically and mentally. Once you come to accept and fully internalize the truth in that connection, you will come to see that with every step you take, you are working to beat back your depression and chart a path to lifelong health.

Many people find additional motivation to increase their walking time by gamifying the activity, either through competing with friends through Fitbit and similar fitness tracker apps or in real life, by meeting up for hikes or regular walks. These choices have the additional benefit of increasing one's social ties and adding the regularity of habit, relieving a portion of the burden of continual self-motivation and reminding oneself to get as much activity as possible. Other people elect to 'compete' with themselves, working to continually better their total number of steps or time spent walking. In either case, if you want to keep track of your walking statistics you may be surprised to find that you may not have to invest even a single additional penny on fitness trackers: many current smartphones keep track of such activities by default, including the widely popular Apple iPhone. However, it should be noted that some people find that such gamifying may exacerbate previously existing tendencies towards anxiety or symptoms of obsessive-compulsive disorder, in which case the tracking should be discontinued—but regardless whether you choose to track and gamify your walking or not, the exercise should be sustained.

Beyond walking, I'm sure it comes as little surprise to you that dozens if not hundreds or thousands of exercise options are currently available, in all ranges of skill from beginning novices to experienced lifelong practitioners. While the scope of this book is too narrow to cover every possible option, you will likely prove the best judge of which activities seem right for you—with the caveat that where possible, in terms of fighting depression it is generally best to select athletic activities which will tend to increase one's social connection and opportunities rather than isolate one further. Boxing, martial arts, dancing, surfing, bicycling, yoga, climbing, water fitness—the range and number of options can seem endless, as well as potentially overwhelming. It can also be all too easy to convince yourself that a particular choice might seem not to be for you before even having tried it based on possibly mistaken preconceptions. I would encourage you to give as many possibilities a try as you can, as each have their unique strengths and benefits. Additionally, it tends to be much, much easier to maintain regular exercise as a part of your life once you manage to find an exercise activity you actually enjoy and look forward to. When it comes to fighting depression, the specific type of exercise is less important than actually making an effort to get exercise, no matter the type—so if you haven't found the type of exercise that's right for you, keep looking.

If you suffer from physical ailments that prevent you from taking part in certain activities, you may justifiably feel more limited in your choices than others. However, as long as you retain the ability to move substantial parts of your body voluntarily, chances are good to excellent you'll be able to discover a workout that works for you. For example, many people with joint problems or other issues with mobility have found swimming and other water-based exercises help lighten the load gravity places upon each of us every day, and by taking advantage of networking platforms such as Meetup.com or programs offered in your community, you should be able to find a supportive group of like-minded individuals without too much trouble. (If in doubt whether your health is sufficient for a certain activity, consult your doctor beforehand.) Finally, even once you've discovered an exercise regimen that works for you, don't feel the need to limit yourself to that exclusively. By changing up your routine, you can break up the monotony, keep yourself motivated, and reap even greater rewards by both exercising your body and keeping depression at bay while entertaining yourself.

No matter what type or types of exercise you settle upon, it is highly advisable to introduce regular stretching into your routine to mitigate built-up tension and soothe stressed muscles, as well as to help boost the depression-fighting effects of your workout. Some exercise regimens like yoga and tai chi incorporate stretching as a major component, of course, but studies have shown that regular stretching alone for as little as ten minutes at a time can have remarkable effects at reducing the symptoms of depression, both by relieving accumulated tension and by helping your body release endorphins. By combining stretching with exercise, you not only increase the depression-fighting effects of both, but help balance out the inevitable soreness that can occur in the wake of a particularly intense workout, preventing yourself from suffering those next-day dull aches and keeping yourself ready to roll the next time your workout rolls around. Light stretching is an excellent way to wind down before bed as well, soothing away the accumulated stresses of the day and clearing your head before you lie down, satisfied that you have done your best to beat back the symptoms of your depression that day, ready to reap the rewards of your well-deserved rest.

But even once you've laid down to sleep, your fight against depression isn't over—sleep itself is a crucial component of the battle against depression and maintaining a depression-free lifestyle. In the next section, we'll take a look at how getting the proper amount of healthy, restful sleep on a regular basis can help alleviate your symptoms of depression.

CHAPTER 6

FIGHTING DEPRESSION WITH SLEEP

AS WE'VE SEEN, the length and quality of one's sleep is closely tied to incidence of depression: either too little or too much sleep, or an inability to fall asleep or stay asleep, can be an important indicator of tendencies toward or symptom of depression. Therefore, it will probably not surprise you that working to manage one's sleep in order to get the most restful sleep possible can be an important factor in the fight against depression.

In today's fast-paced world, it can be all too tempting to short oneself of necessary sleeping hours, whether to meet the burdens of a demanding job, to take advantage of late-night social opportunities, or simply to catch up on television shows that everyone else seems to be talking about. However, studies have shown that this can have devastating emotional effects, particularly over extended periods of time: in fact, compared to those who manage the typical seven to nine hours of sleep per night, people who get five or fewer hours of sleep nightly are doubly at risk of developing depression. If you count yourself among those who are already at risk for depressive symptoms, it's likely unwise to deprive yourself of restful hours more frequently than the occasional unavoidable short night—and if you are sleeping no more than five or six hours a night while currently suffering from depression, you owe it to yourself to begin taking steps to change your sleep habits as soon as possible.

Unfortunately, lack of quality sleep and depression are so intricately linked that even for experts, in certain cases it can be difficult to determine which condition is the cause of the other. Sleep apnea, a widespread disorder of breathing disruption during sleep, has been directly linked to incidence of depression, as have several other sleep ailments such as chronic insomnia, hypersomnia (excessive sleepiness or oversleeping), and restless legs syndrome. Problems sleeping regularly or getting enough restful sleep can also inhibit any attempts to recover from the symptoms of depression by preventing the sufferer from exercising regularly or otherwise recuperating from the negative effects of their condition. As a result, those who suffer both from severe depression and frequent sleep disruption may require the assistance of a medical professional to determine which condition is the root cause before addressing either.

Short of consulting a sleep clinic or other medical authority, however, there are many steps one can take on their own in order to improve both quantity and quality of sleep. As with fitness, a number of sleep trackers are now available to help keep tabs on your sleep cycles, allowing you to maintain hard data on your sleep over time and make adjustments accordingly; by using such devices you may be able to fine-tune your nighttime routine to that most optimal for restful sleep. Caffeine, alcohol, and nicotine use should be avoided during the evening, as all three substances can cause trouble sleeping or difficulty getting restful sleep—and those depression sufferers whose symptoms include physical pain such as back pain or headaches should take care to note that many over-the-counter pain relievers contain large amounts of caffeine as part of their chemical makeup, so be sure to check the bottle prior to dosing yourself directly before bed.

Activities such as meditation, guided imagery, hypnotherapy, stretching, deep breathing, and light yoga may help relax you and ease your passage into dreamland; taking a warm shower before bed has also been shown to encourage deep sleep as the body cools. If your bedroom is subject to intrusive light or sound, either from within your household or outside, blackout curtains and white noise generators can help create a soothing environment that encourages healthy, natural sleep patterns. Short of those options, a sleep mask and earplugs may produce similar results, and an ordinary household fan can also substitute as an effective and practical white noise generator. Aromatic oils might also help to create the relaxing, sleep-promoting environment your bedroom should be, as your sanctuary of rest. If your bed itself is old, worn, or otherwise nonideal, it might also be worth considering the benefits of switching to a newer, more comfortable surface on which to rest— recently, discount mattresses have begun to be offered even through mail-order services, so it is entirely likely you will be able to locate such an upgrade more affordably than previously thought. It may also help to mentally designate the bed for sleeping and sexual activity only, subconsciously linking the bed solely with sleeping rather than associating it with activities such as watching television, reading, eating, playing games, or any of the many other leisure activities that are now possible without getting out of bed.

Recently, the increased proliferation of computer screens of various kinds and their ubiquity in our lives has led to an uptick in sleep disorders among many people. It is thought that the increased exposure to certain frequencies of light produced by smartphones, tablet or laptop computers, and television screens can make it more difficult for some people to fall asleep readily by inhibiting the brain from releasing melatonin, a natural hormone which signals the body that sleep is imminent. As a result, many such electronic devices offer a 'night shift' option in which blue light frequencies are reduced, creating a 'warmer' feel and ideally, mini-mizing the sleep-disrupting qualities of these devices. However, it should be noted that at this time, most evidence regarding the efficacy of such color shifting is anecdotal at best. If you are serious about reducing the potential effects of such screens upon your sleep patterns, it would likely be better to simply ensure such screens are either shut off or not used within your view at least an hour before attempting to sleep. If you like to read before bed, as many do, consider limiting yourself to books and magazines on paper before bedtime.

In general, the use of sleeping pills and other pharmacolog-ical sleep aids is not recommended for those with depres-sion. Such substances often do not elicit the desired amount of restful sleep and can also lead to addictive tendencies, both of which are counterproductive in the struggle against depression. In extreme cases, such drugs might be adminis-tered to help a patient overcome severe difficulty resting, particularly following recent trauma or to augment the effects of a prescribed antidepressant, but for the most part these medicines should only be used under the supervision of a medical professional. In the battle against depression, most will find the best result and the greatest alleviation of their depressive symptoms not by resorting to pharmacological sleep aids, but by modifying their behavior in order to maximize the amount of natural sleep they are able to achieve each night. By doing so, not only will the day's struggles seem less onerous and depression symptoms be reduced in intensity, but by recognizing the importance of rest on our waking hours we reinforce healthy sleep habits and help build patterns designed to keep depression at bay for life.

Strangely, while lack of sleep is generally associated with increased depression, in certain cases controlled sleep deprivation has been shown to lessen depressive symptoms. While this might seem counterintuitive, it is thought that performing this type of structured manipulation of the sleep cycle—typically consisting of a day or two of supervised sleep deprivation, followed by several days of adjusting one's sleep schedule according to predefined times—may serve as a type of shock to the body's circadian rhythms, allowing one to reset poor sleep habits, get used to healthier sleep patterns, and lessen depressive symptoms.

Unfortunately, in most cases this reduction of depressive symptoms generally proves temporary, often returning within one week. Further, becoming accustomed to new and different sleep habits is frequently more a byproduct of making conscious choices and adhering to a disciplined sleep schedule over time, rather than making abrupt adjustments to the body's rhythms. This type of treatment is also discouraged in the elderly as well as those suffering from cognitive impairment, so should not be considered an option in such cases. However, for those who face extreme difficulty in reorienting their sleep cycles to healthier hours even after many attempts, it may be worth considering the potential benefits to be derived from such treatment; if so, consult a local sleep clinic or your doctor for more information.

CHAPTER 7

FIGHTING DEPRESSION WITH SUNLIGHT

WHILE MOST PEOPLE today are aware of the potential
negative effects of too much exposure to sunlight in terms of
increased risk of sun damage and other skin conditions,
fewer realize that lack of exposure to the sun's rays can pack
a devastating emotional impact. Because sunlight exposure
is tied directly to production of serotonin, a neurotransmitter linked to mood and appetite, increased exposure to
sunlight can often have an antidepressive effect. In fact,
many popular prescription antidepressants function specifically by affecting the body's production and reception of
serotonin; these substances are therefore referred to as selective serotonin reuptake inhibitors, or SSRIs for short.

Lack of sunlight exposure has also been tied to seasonal
affective disorder, or SAD, which is believed to be triggered
by the fluctuation of sunlight hours during months of the
year with reduced exposure to the sun's rays, desynchro-
nizing a person's waking schedule away from the natural
hours of daylight and eventually producing depression.
Symptoms similar to seasonal affective disorder can also be

activated in people who regularly work second or third shifts and tend to sleep during daylight hours, therefore limiting their potential exposure to daylight during waking hours and causing sleep disruption due to daylight exposure when sleeping—a double blow to healthy rest. Additionally, such working patterns can also inhibit attempts to recover from other depressive symptoms by limiting socialization, participation in exercise programs, and otherwise encouraging isolation, both physical and emotional.

Increasing time of exposure to the sun during what daylight hours exist during such times can help mitigate these problems, aided by supplementation by artificial sun lamps or light boxes during times when the sun's rays simply aren't around. Typically, the effects of seasonal affective disorder tend to diminish and eventually vanish as the seasons turn back toward months with more hours of sunlight, but in more severe cases more aggressive forms of treatment may prove necessary. For depression sufferers who work nighttime hours and suffer depressive symptoms as a result, career changes might be required; if a current job does not allow for a switch to working during daytime hours or cycling on and off of nighttime workdays, a more desirable position may need to be located in order to recover a long-term healthy mindset.

Of course, where the sun's rays are concerned, more is not necessarily better—sun exposure can be unhealthy in excessive doses and should be limited to the amount necessary to produce the desired results. In general, people with lighter skin will have much less tolerance to the sun's rays, and should be especially conscious to limit their contact with the sun's rays so as to prevent increased incidence of sun damage and a heightened risk of skin cancers, but while less common, these conditions can certainly affect people with darker skin as well. For these reasons, long hours in the sun are generally not advisable for anyone, no matter their skin color or diligence in applying sunscreen.

Beyond the sun's effects on the body's serotonin production, however, its rays also serve as our primary source of vitamin D. And as you might guess, the changes in human lifestyle that took us away from the sun's rays have also led to widespread vitamin D deficiencies. In the next section, we'll take a look at how these and other nutrient deficiencies have contributed to the epidemic spread of depression, along with how we can help mitigate those effects by making changes in our diet to adjust the levels of depression-fighting vitamins, minerals, and other nutrients we ingest.

CHAPTER 8

FIGHTING DEPRESSION WITH FOOD, VITAMINS, AND NUTRIENTS

MORE AND MORE, we are becoming aware of how the foods we consume contribute not only to our overall health or lack of same, but also affect our mental state and moods on an ongoing, lifelong basis. In retrospect, it seems almost strange to think that people once believed we could consume virtually anything with impunity, but the truth is now apparent that different foods produce widely varying reactions in the human body, including direct links to mood and sleep disorders, along with comprising one of the most important factors in long-term health.

No, this doesn't necessarily mean you'll have to completely give up your favorite comfort foods in order to effectively fight your depression, at least outside of certain highly unlikely circumstances. But if you're suffering from depression, you can definitely reduce the frequency and intensity of your symptoms significantly by beginning to make healthier, smarter choices as of right now—and by doing so, you will be less likely to experience the familiar spiral of guilt, sadness, and self-loathing that can so often follow in the wake of a junk food bender.

That's not to say that the effects of comfort food are to be entirely dismissed, however. That temporary 'lift' in mood you quite likely experience after eating a longtime favorite snack is a very real effect that has been documented in many clinical tests. However, this effect has also been demonstrated to be exceedingly temporary in duration. Worse, as many comfort foods tend to be rich in refined sugar or other carbohydrates, that lift is nearly always followed by a crash of equal or greater proportions, particularly when overindulgence comes into play. The key with comfort foods is to use them very sparingly as motivational rewards for making real progress towards your goals, thus providing an additional, immediately tangible reward for working towards beating your depression, as well as to understand that while you should not berate yourself for spoiling yourself with the occasional nonessential treat, you should realize that by doing so you are also not making positive steps forward to conquer your depression. And frankly, if you are 'rewarding' yourself nearly every day, well—that's not a reward, that's a habit.

Additionally, while we can safely make some generalizations regarding how certain foods tend to affect the human body, different people can occasionally react in different ways to the same diet. For example, those with celiac disease, which is estimated to affect approximately one in a hundred people worldwide, carry not only a severe intolerance for gluten which can be safely digested by the other ninety-nine percent of the population, but also an eighty percent higher risk of depression. These idiosyncratic variations can depend on a number of factors, including body chemistry and family history, as well as allergic reactions, weight, and the effects of prescribed medication. As a result, there is as of yet no single anti-depression diet that has been demonstrated to be universally effective; where treating your depression with food and nutrition is concerned, there is currently little recourse but to test out a number of options and discover through trial and error which works best for you personally and your lifestyle.

However, while variations in human digestion exist, certain factors are near universal. No matter who you are, it's likely that controlling your carbohydrate intake will be a significant component of your own personal anti-depression diet: high-glycemic diets have been shown to increase likelihood of developing depression, particularly in the elderly, and fast food consumption has been directly correlated with depression. Ironically, worldwide consumption of refined sugars and simple carbohydrates has skyrocketed along with the spread of the sedentary lifestyle which largely makes the need for consuming such foodstuffs obsolete and irrelevant. While your taste buds may tell you that you need that doughnut lovingly crafted from refined white flour and two kinds of sugar in the morning, chances are slim to none that during the rest of the day you'll be performing the type of strenuous physical activity necessary to justify such a nutrient-deficient breakfast. Worse, recent studies have demonstrated links between increased consumption of refined carbohydrates and a heightened risk of depression, as well as an association between low levels of serotonin and recurrent cravings for refined carbohydrates—so for those who already suffer from depression, these refined carbs might be getting you both coming and going. Unfortunately, the serotonin boost provided by carb indulgence fades far more quickly than the caloric load that refined snack delivers. And if that isn't bad enough, people who experience those aforementioned carbohydrate cravings are estimated to consume an extra eight hundred calories per day compared to average—almost none of which contributes to overall health in any way, and the majority of which is likely only to be stored by the body as fat.

Instead of indulging your craving for refined carbohydrate treats—most of which contain virtually no healthy nutrients—whenever possible, you should opt for complex carbohydrates such as those provided by whole grains, brown rice, legumes, and wheat pasta, rather than the simple carbohydrates contained in white bread, white rice, and traditional pasta, as well as nearly all the sugary snacks on your grocery's shelves. And while you don't have to immediately dive into a low-carb diet lifestyle such as that advocated by Dr. Robert Atkins, it might be worth investigating how such diets affect your particular body chemistry, as some people do experience satisfying weight loss and decreased incidence of depression by drastically reducing their daily overall carbohydrate intake. Others should opt for snacks with more balanced levels of both carbohydrates and protein, which can help counteract the 'carbohydrate crash' effect by providing longer-lasting energy, such as yogurt, skim milk, or cheese and wheat crackers. No matter your personal chemistry, by taking steps to minimize empty junk food and other foods containing high levels of simple carbohydrates, you can attain a balanced blood sugar and not only help control your depression, but also keep your weight down and minimize your risks for developing diabetes.

Beyond carbohydrates, a wide range of vitamins and other

nutrients have also been linked to depression in various ways. Omega-3 acids, which help in construction of brain cells and building connections between them, are referred to as essential fatty acids because the human body is incapable of synthesizing them; therefore, they must be derived entirely from food intake, despite being necessary for maintaining good health. Primarily derived from oily fish such as salmon, sardines, tuna, and trout, omega-3 fatty acid deficiencies are so closely correlated with depression that studies have indicated that significantly lower levels of depression exist in cultures which consume more fish as part of their regular diet. Additionally, for much of human history prior to the development of modern farming techniques, our ancestors regularly ate much higher concentrations of omega-3 than we do today, as wild fish and game contains much higher levels than farm-raised meat. Unfortunately for depression sufferers who wish to adhere to a strictly vegetarian diet, absorption of omega-3 is much greater from animal-derived sources; however, walnuts, flaxseed, and hemp seeds all provide significant levels of omega-3 for those who eschew or limit consumption of meat. Either way, while it is generally better to derive your nutrients from food rather than supplements, if you have difficulty obtaining optimal levels of omega-3 from your diet alone, omega-3 supplementation might be advisable—particularly for women who are pregnant or nursing, as such individuals have been shown to be particularly susceptible to omega-3 deficiency-based depression.

Deficiencies in regular intake of folic acid or B9, an essential B vitamin, have similarly been linked to tendencies toward depression. In a number of studies, about one-third of subjects suffering from depression were determined to be folate deficient. Further, though depression patients who suffered from low levels of folic acid have been shown to be less likely to show significant improvement when administered anti-depressant SSRI medicines, the percentage of patients indicating improved results jumped to ninety-three percent when SSRIs were supplemented with folic acid. Fortunately, folic acid is much easier to add to most people's diet than omega-3 acids: readily obtained from green leafy vegetables such as spinach and brussels sprouts, as well as tomatoes, asparagus, avocado, beef liver, beans, and lentils, B9 is also widely added to bread and other grain products in many areas in order to alleviate chronic folate deficiencies among the population. As a result, by paying attention to the nutrition information on the food you typically buy you should be able to lift your folate consumption levels fairly easily without requiring additional supplementation—but if you do, try to get it from healthy, natural sources such as the aforementioned green leafy vegetables before resorting to mass-produced supplement pills.

Along with B9, deficiencies in other B vitamins such as vitamins B6 and B12 have been connected to depression. In fact, a B12 deficiency alone can produce remarkably depression-like symptoms, without any other contributing factors whatsoever. Both B6 and B12 are essential to the formation of serotonin and dopamine, neurotransmitters known to affect mood; B6 additionally aids in metabolizing both glycogen and amino acids, while B12 is crucial for construction of red blood cells and the nerves' fatty layer. Though B6 is widely available in a number of foods, including poultry, fish, green leafy vegetables, bananas and chickpeas, B12 is only available from animal-derived sources, particularly seafood, beef, and lamb. For this reason, anyone eating a vegetarian or vegan diet should regularly accompany their food intake with a B12 supplement, whether currently suffering from symptoms of depression or not. Conditions such as celiac disease, Crohn's disease, recent weight loss surgery, or reaching ages over fifty may also make it more difficult to ingest sufficient levels of B12 because of changes in the way the body extracts and absorbs nutrients from food; if you fall into any of the above categories, you might want to consider B12 supplementation as well.

As alluded to in the previous chapter, vitamin D deficiency has become so common that some are referring to it as a major epidemic. Because sunlight is our major source of vitamin D, producing around ninety percent of our daily supply, it doesn't take much consideration to recognize how changes in human lifestyle over the past hundred and fifty years have led to this state: many of us work inside artificially-lit buildings in front of computers all day long, only seeing the sun for brief instants when walking to and from our vehicles—and in winter months, perhaps not even then. Unluckily, along with decreased exposure to the sun has come increased knowledge of the negative effects of the sun's rays, justifiably making many people leery to spend more time exposed to the sun than absolutely necessary. Even then, people with dark skin, the elderly, and overweight people will tend to require significantly more sun exposure to derive the same amount of vitamin D from the sun's rays as a young, light-skinned person of healthy weight, and relatively few people eat large amounts of fatty fish like tuna, salmon, and mackerel—the best food-based source of vitamin D—on a daily basis. In such cases, daily supplementation is highly recommended to bolster the body's vitamin D supply without increasing risks due to excessive sun exposure. Fortunately, because vitamin D deficiency is so pervasive and well known, the nutrient is added as a supplement to a wide range of foods such as dairy products, cereal, orange juice, and soy milk, among others, so maintaining sufficient vitamin D levels should not be difficult.

Because the abovementioned vitamin deficiencies are widespread and have become relatively recognized, you should be able to locate a multivitamin supplement to cover your requirements relatively easily by checking the labels at your local grocery, drug store, or health food store. By doing so, you can be sure you're getting the recommended daily allowance of any number of depression-fighting vitamins and minerals, along with many others to help bolster and maintain your immune system and overall long term health. If you have doubts about which of the many multivitamin supplements on the market may be right for you—formulations can vary widely for various groups, including women, men, kids, teenagers, and the elderly—consult a nutritionist or doctor.

Magnesium deficiency has become similarly frequent, with some estimates placing the level of Americans suffering chronically low levels of magnesium as high as fifty percent. Widely available from food sources such as green leafy vegetables, nuts including almonds and cashews, as well as beans and legumes, some recent experimental studies have indicated magnesium supplementation may serve as an effective anti-depressant in certain conditions. However, it should be noted that the levels of magnesium supplementation used in these studies were higher than is generally considered safe for human consumption on a regular basis.

Further, elevated levels of magnesium can produce a range of negative effects ranging from confusion, low blood pressure, and irregular heartbeat all the way up to coma or even death in extreme cases. As a result, magnesium supplementation should not be given to children, nor to people with kidney problems, as proper kidney functioning is necessary for proper elimination of excess magnesium. Additionally, under certain conditions the body's demand for magnesium may be higher than normal, including pregnancy, intense athletic training, and recovery from surgery, and magnesium supplementation may interact with other medications and supplements such as antibiotics, diuretics, muscle relaxers, vitamin D, calcium, and zinc. For these reasons, if you wish to introduce magnesium supplementation into your routine in order to help in your fight against depression, you should consult a doctor who is aware of your medical history and any other medications and supplements you might be taking regularly in order to determine the proper level of magnesium for you. Otherwise, making an effort to eat the proper foods on a regular basis should suffice to meet your daily magnesium needs.

Iron deficiency, while not widely considered a major cause of depression, might well be a contributing factor in certain cases—particularly in women, who suffer such deficiencies in overwhelmingly greater numbers than men. It is estimated that while only three percent of men have iron deficiencies, about twenty percent of women and as much as fifty percent of pregnant women do not get sufficient iron in their diet. This lack of iron results in a decline in the body's ability to create red blood cells, causing an inability to process enough oxygen and eventually leading to anemia, which carries depression as one of its major symptoms, along with irritability, chronic fatigue, mood swings, lack of appetite, difficulty concentrating, and headaches. Therefore, women who have addressed other potential causes for depression and still suffer from its effects might do well to get themselves checked for anemia, as well as to increase their daily intake of iron through regular consumption of foods like red meat, poultry and fish. Vegetarians may opt for high-iron sources like squash and pumpkin seeds, the ever-present dark leafy greens, or iron supplements; often, women's multivitamins include substantially higher doses of iron than multivitamins intended for men, specifically to address this frequently-seen deficiency.

Zinc is an often-ignored trace mineral which serves a crucial part in over a hundred enzymatic reactions, working to activate digestive enzymes, prevent food allergies, bolster the immune system, and control inflammation, among other important functions. While the mass of evidence linking zinc deficiencies with depression is still relatively low, a number of studies have demonstrated low levels of zinc both in depressed patients and the elderly, improved remediation of depressive symptoms in subjects administered zinc supplementation along with SSRI antidepressants in double-blind placebo-controlled trials, and reduction in symptoms of post-natal depression in pregnant women with higher zinc levels. A number of theories regarding zinc's role in fighting and preventing depression exist, one of the most prominent being that because of zinc's important role in maintaining proper digestive function, a zinc deficiency may prevent the gastrointestinal system from properly processing the many other substances that have been directly shown to affect mood; another proffered theory postulates that low levels of zinc are tied in with the immune system and inflammatory reactions that comprise the body's attempt to eliminate pathogens through elevated body temperature. Whatever the truth, the correlation between insufficient zinc levels and depressive symptoms is cause for notice by those wishing to fight depression. Most widely found in beef, lamb, shellfish and poultry, zinc can also be derived from plant-based sources such as whole grains, nuts, and seeds, though unfortunately bioavailability of zinc from plant sources can be distressingly low—as little as fifteen percent. For this reason, depressive vegetarians who suspect they may be suffering from a zinc deficiency may choose to augment their diet with zinc supplements, though care should be taken not to exceed levels of around fifty milligrams per day, as high doses of zinc can cause symptoms of acute toxicity.

Selenium, another trace mineral essential to good health, has also been shown to lessen symptoms of postpartum depression in women, as well as to help lower incidence of depression among the elderly. Found in its highest concentrations in Brazil nuts, selenium can also be derived from poultry, seafood, eggs, and whole grains, though its presence in grains produced in certain areas may be lower due to lack of selenium in the soil. While low levels of selenium have been linked to depressive symptoms and negative effects on mood, higher concentrations of selenium were also linked to poor mood within the same studies. Further, excessively high selenium levels have been associated with increased risks of diabetes, and toxicity can be reached with surprisingly small amounts of selenium—as low as a milligram. For these reasons, before supplementing with high doses of selenium consider the amount you are ingesting from your current diet, and take a cautious approach when adding selenium-rich foods to your daily routine. Because Brazil nuts are so high in selenium, most experts suggest simply consuming one or two daily to safely bolster your selenium intake without running a risk of reaching dangerous levels.

Chromium, another essential mineral found in whole grains, mushrooms, brewer's yeast, and liver, helps regulate the blood sugar and metabolize fats, carbohydrates, and proteins. Because of this, many people with diabetes or prediabetic symptoms are given chromium supplementation to help their systems process these substances properly —but perhaps also as a result, chromium has been shown to help curb carbohydrate cravings and stabilize mood in depressed people. While this does not indicate all individuals suffering from depression should supplement their diets with chromium, if you suffer from the particular form of depression that comes with intense, repeated carbohydrate cravings, chromium might well help remediate your symptoms as well as work to help prevent you from developing diabetes later in life.

Assuming you've been paying close attention through this book so far, you'll likely not be surprised that depleted levels of the neurotransmitter serotonin have been closely linked to incidence of depression, given that many prescription antidepressants primarily function by affecting these serotonin levels. If so, you may have quite reasonably asked yourself: if this is so, why not supplement with serotonin directly, cutting out the middleman and getting straight to the point? The reason for this is that we can't—ingested serotonin is unable to cross the blood-brain barrier and therefore will not affect the mind's functioning—but we can supplement with nutrients that produce elevated serotonin levels, such as tryptophan, an amino acid that serves as an immediate precursor to production of serotonin. Tryptophan, of course, is widely known to be found in turkey, and due to popular misconception is often blamed for the sleepy feeling people often have following Thanksgiving dinner—as if the relatively minor effects of the tryptophan contained in turkey superceded the massive carbohydrate load that accompanied it. While the sedative properties of tryptophan are largely exaggerated, this essential amino acid does work as a natural relaxant, helping to mitigate anxiety, and as it converts to serotonin which then converts to melatonin, supplementing with tryptophan can indeed help normalize your sleep patterns. Because of this, it is frequently used to treat sleep disorders, but whether or not you suffer from sleep disruption, supplementing with tryptophan to address a serotonin deficiency may well prove an effective treatment for your symptoms of depression, without the unpleasant side effects that can come along with prescription antidepressants. However, if you are currently taking any prescription SSRI medicine, tryptophan supplementation should be avoided in order to prevent interactions; in effect, doubling up on controlling your serotonin levels by using both substances simultaneously may produce undesirable effects referred to as 'serotonin syndrome', symptoms of which include high body temperature, diarrhea, agitation, and dilated pupils. If you have any doubt whether you are using prescription drugs which might affect serotonin production, consult your doctor before adding tryptophan to your diet.

Other amino acids such as tyrosine, glutamine, and phenylalanine have also been demonstrated to boost serotonin, along with other mood-affecting neurotransmitters such as dopamine, epinephrine, norepinephrine, and adrenaline.

Because finding the proper balance of amino acid supplementation for each individual can largely be a matter of trial-and-error guesswork based upon their own unique body chemistry and environmental factors, it might be best for those considering extensive amino acid therapy to do so under the advice of an expert such as their doctor. If you do choose to experiment with amino acid supplements, do so conservatively, beginning with small doses and judging the effects over a significant period of time before adding different types of supplementation or increasing your regular dosages.

If you've paid any attention to health food news over the past decade, you've likely already heard about antioxidants: compounds found naturally in a wide range of fruits and vegetables that help protect cells from damage caused by oxidative stress. While a few studies have indicated low levels of antioxidants in patients being treated for depression, there is as of yet little indication of a causative relationship. While patients who ingested more antioxidant-containing fruits and vegetables did display significantly improved symptoms, those selfsame fruits and vegetables also contained several other substances that have been more conclusively demonstrated to have direct effects upon mood—as you no doubt already realize after having gotten this far through this chapter. Additionally, adding antioxidants to patients' diets in supplement form failed to produce similar results, casting doubt upon any potential direct connection between antioxidant levels and depression. However, if you do wish to raise your own antioxidant levels through consumption of antioxidant-rich foods such as walnuts, berries, broccoli, and tomatoes, you are hardly likely to either do yourself harm or to worsen your depression—as noted, the other nutrients contained therein are very likely to improve both your depressive symptoms and overall long term health—just don't be so quick to attribute those positive results to the antioxidants.

While there any many theories about how depression affects the body, one that has gained much traction in recent years characterizes ongoing depression as a system-wide inflammation. Elevated markers of inflammation have been noted in depressed patients, and some pro-inflammatory medicines have led to unexpected levels of depression when administered. For this reason, some suggest that maintaining an anti-inflammatory diet or taking anti-inflammatory medication might help lessen depressive symptoms as well as lower the risk of developing depression, particularly as the aging process progresses. At this point, however, the connections remain indeterminate—even the drug companies developing potential anti-inflammatory depression medications caution that they will likely remain reserved for those who fail to respond to other treatment. Still, much like antioxidants, those who wish to follow anti-inflammatory diets and lifestyles are unlikely to do themselves harm: among the most widely suggested anti-inflammatory recommendations are to consume fewer refined carbohydrates, sugar, and sodium; eating more nuts, green leafy vegetables, seafood, and berries; and lowering stress, getting regular exercise, and getting the proper amount of sleep. Considering these suggestions line up almost perfectly with the most widely accepted choices you can make to relieve depression, deciding to follow an anti-inflammatory diet and lifestyle might be as effective a choice as any.

The remaining suggestions and recommendations for depression-fighting food and nutrient choices beyond this point may produce diminishing returns, as most conclusions are too premature or disparate to effectively judge one way or another. As more evidence comes in, the roles these substances do or do not play in depression will inevitably become more clear, but for now, it's simply too early to make blanket determinations one way or another.

No substance demonstrates this lack of consensus more clearly than caffeine, one of the most widely consumed drugs in the world. While some studies have suggested a depression-fighting effect to regular consumption of coffee and other caffeinated beverages, other have indicated precisely the opposite, along with tendencies for caffeine to stimulate anxiety, headaches, and high blood pressure, as well as to reduce serotonin levels. After taking caffeine's well-known ability to disrupt natural sleep patterns into account, it seems difficult to recommend highly-caffeinated beverages as a remedy for symptoms of depression—though it is suggested that if you are already consuming four or more cups per day, chances are high you are attempting to self-medicate your system, perhaps without even being aware of it. If you do not presently ingest much caffeine, beginning now is unlikely to lead to a long term reduction in your depression symptoms. Conversely, if you consume caffeine as a regular part of your routine, quitting suddenly may lead to a worsening of your symptoms until your system adjusts. Instead, try gradually reducing your caffeine intake and never consume caffeine less than four hours before bed.

In food and nutrition circles, artificial sweeteners constitute a frequent, if not constant, topic of controversy. As such, it is hardly surprising to find that some have attempted to draw correlations between depression and the consumption of sweeteners such as aspartame, sucralose, and saccharin. While one study did suggest a tie between consumption of artificially sweetened diet drinks and increased incidence of depression, no cause and effect relationship was established therein. Additionally, many researchers have pointed to any number of additional factors that might have easily explained the results, such as the fact that people prone to other depression-causing conditions such as diabetes and obesity are much more likely than average to consume diet drinks, along with the telling point that the selfsame study found identical results from sugar-sweetened drinks, casting severe doubt on artificial sweeteners being the inarguable root of the problem. While as of yet, no credible research has established any certain negative effects from consumption of such sweeteners, the debate rages on; that being the case, any number of claims have been (and will likely continue to be) made regarding the long-term impact of these substances. However, no matter which way it shakes out in the long run, one thing is absolutely certain: regardless of their potential health impact, no artificial sweeteners provide any nutrients of substance whatsoever. Therefore, if you wish to cut such sweeteners out of your diet for any reason, whether depression-linked or not, you stand to lose little by replacing such sweetened products with healthier alternatives—as long as you don't resort to conventional sugar-sweetened treats, which, as we have seen, have definite and well-established negative effects.

Chocolate is another popular sweet treat that has been tied to depression in a wide range of contradictory ways. While some have suggested an antidepressant effect may be produced by chocolate consumption, a recent study indicated that those who consumed more chocolate were significantly more likely to be depressed than those who ate less—and the more chocolate they ate, the more severe their depression symptoms. However, again no cause-and-effect relationship was established, and it was postulated that perhaps the depression symptoms triggered the chocolate cravings, rather than vice versa. Further, it should be noted that the overwhelming majority of chocolate products contain high levels of sugar and other highly refined carbohydrates, as well as caffeine and any number of additives, fillers, and preservatives. Therefore, while the occasional chocolate indulgence might provide a temporary lift in your spirits, more than that is unlikely to produce positive results in your fight against depression.

The spice saffron was traditionally used to treat depression along with a number of other conditions in traditional Persian medicine, but clinical research into saffron's effects has only recently started being conducted. Initial findings seem promising, however, with one study finding regular dosing with saffron tablets produced a reduction in depression symptoms comparable with some prescription antidepressants, without the potential negative side effects of SSRI prescription drugs. While much future investigation is necessary to determine factors such as long-term effects, effective dosages, and duration of treatment before saffron is widely accepted and used to treat depression, these early findings certainly merit keeping a cautiously optimistic eye on this research as it progresses. Unfortunately, the most serious obstacle to widespread saffron use in this area may well be its cost: because it must be delicately harvested by hand, saffron can retail for as much as eleven thousand dollars per kilogram and is popularly referred to as the most expensive spice in the world. For this reason, saffron may not be an ideal choice for most people wishing to assuage their depression symptoms, but if more information becomes available and further studies continue to support saffron's efficacy in depression treatment, in the future the spice may well become more widespread—and hopefully, significantly less expensive.

S-adenosylmethionine, or SAMe, is a naturally occurring molecular compound which has been used in Europe for some time to treat depression, along with a range of other conditions including arthritis, attention deficit hyperactivity disorder or ADHD, premenstrual syndrome or PMS, liver disease, and fibromyalgia. Knowledge and use of SAMe supplementation is still in its early stages elsewhere, however, and its efficacy has not been conclusively deter-mined one way or another, nor has precisely how the substance functions been established. Its over thirty-year history of European usage does provide some reassurance of concerns over potential long-term effects, though it has been indicated to worsen manic symptoms and cause gastroin-testinal upset in some. Furthermore, studies indicate SAMe requires sufficient levels of folate along with vitamins B_{12} and B6 in order to produce positive results—substances that you might recall as having been demonstrated to have a positive effect on mood on their own. Fortunately, anecdotal evidence suggests the effects of SAMe may manifest within a few days, rather than the weeks or longer some antidepres-sant substances can take to produce remediation, so should you choose to experiment with SAMe supplementation to fight your depression, it shouldn't take long to discover whether or not it works for you. If you decide to experiment with effects of SAMe, do so cautiously by beginning with small doses and consulting your doctor beforehand, particularly if you are currently taking prescription antidepressants, which have been reported to interact negatively with SAMe by producing undesirably high levels of serotonin.

Finally, St. John's Wort is a widely known herbal supplement used by a number of people for many reasons, among which is the treatment of depression. Due to its popularity, a number of studies have been performed testing the efficacy of St. John's Wort when used to remediate depressive symptoms, with overall positive results in reducing symptoms of mild to moderate depression, although subjects exhibiting major depression generally reported no improvement. Unfortunately, St. Johns' Wort has also been shown to produce a number of negative effects from interactions with many other drugs, including birth control pills, antihistamines, cough suppressants, HIV treatments and other drugs that affect the immune system, sedatives, antifungal medications, and Xanax, along with prescription antidepressants. Use of St. John's Wort supplements has also been linked to increased sensitivity to the sun's rays, as well as decreased fertility and possible worsening of conditions like ADHD, schizophrenia, and dementia. As a result, if you decide to supplement with St. John's Wort, you should do so under the direction of a doctor, particularly if you are currently taking any prescription medication. Despite being a popular herbal remedy, St. John's Wort is not necessarily safer than prescription drugs, particularly since herbal supplements are not regulated by the FDA for quality, purity, or safety. In fact, if you do choose to add St. John's Wort or other herbal supplements to your diet, your biggest problem may be ascertaining whether the supplement you bought actually contains any of the product listed on the label—recent studies have shown that when tested, many herbal products actually contained little to none of the advertised product, instead consisting primarily of fillers like wheat, soy, or rice, while others contained unlisted prescription drugs. For these reasons, anyone wishing to add St. John's Wort or other herbal supplements to their diet should do so with caution.

CHAPTER 9

FIGHTING DEPRESSION WITH FRIENDS, FAMILY, AND LOVED ONES

WHILE MANY DO NOT THINK of loneliness as a disease or medical condition, more and more studies are beginning to indicate that perhaps we should treat it as seriously as one. Elderly people who don't get sufficient social interaction have been shown to be twice as likely to die prematurely as those who enjoy regular and rewarding social contact—a comparable increase in risk as that associated with smoking. In fact, social isolation is roughly twice as hazardous as obesity and comes along with demonstrable physical effects, lowering the effectiveness of the immune system and causing inflammation. Worse, despite the increasingly interconnected world we live in, loneliness is on the rise: while only twenty percent of adults reported feeling lonely during studies conducted in the nineteen-eighties, recent studies place that figure as high as forty percent—a one hundred percent increase in less than forty years. Half of Americans claim to have no close friends outside their immediate family, and one in four Americans report having absolutely no one in whom they can confide whatsoever—a grim scenario, even for an individual not already suffering from depression. If any medical condition carrying such serious implications had undergone a similar increase during such a short time, we'd be discussing it in terms of an epidemic or public health crisis. Yet, when it comes to loneliness, it can often be difficult to admit suffering its effects, even to oneself.

It will likely surprise you little to find that loneliness is a definite risk factor for depression. In both males and females, depression and loneliness have been shown to be linked in approximately equal numbers, indicating that virtually everyone who lacks sufficient social interaction is at risk for developing depression, and vice versa. Assuming you have read this book in order, it will also likely surprise you little to find that as recently as a couple of hundred years ago, this type of social isolation was exceedingly rare. For most of human history, people lived in intimate, tightly connected communities of hunters and gatherers, and where such communities still exist today, loneliness and social isolation are virtually unknown among them—much like depression. But as the majority of humanity has progressed into the modern lifestyle of long commutes, working in boxed-off cubicles facing electronic screens, and social networking primarily through corporate-controlled platforms and apps, that sense of interconnectivity has inevitably withered, along with our collective sense of community and individual importance.

Because most of us have grown up within these circumstances, we consider them normal—but make no mistake that compared to the majority of human history, the times we live in are extreme and strange indeed. The physical systems our bodies have evolved over millions of years to cope with the types of problems humans historically faced are ill suited to deal with issues of social isolation and loneliness, precisely because such issues rarely arose in the past. And when we feel disconnected from this modern way of life, we may feel tempted to in turn attempt to disconnect from it—but in the end, we might only exacerbate our isolation, creating a spiral it can be challenging to negotiate our way free of.

People become isolated by a number of factors, many of which they may feel they have little control over. However, by becoming aware of the problems that come along with isolation and loneliness, we can motivate ourselves to overcome these causes through making small changes and recognizing choices that pop up nearly every day. No, we may not be able to conquer persistent feelings of isolation in a single day, because we cannot construct an entire social support system between sunup and sundown. But by making social contact with other people regularly and creating habitual behaviors, over the course of a few weeks we can begin to break down the seemingly insurmountable barriers society has constructed between individuals and recognize them for what they are—unnatural, easily dissolved walls keeping us from helping one another.

How have we become so isolated? At root, most of the notions that have led us to this point come from one well-intentioned instinct: that of self-preservation and protection. Among our most powerful natural urges, the instinct to protect yourself from pain is among the first we develop as children—yet over time, this instinct has become hypersensitized by the overstimulation of the modern world. In times long past, our sense of potential danger would quite rightly be triggered by meeting strangers or otherwise encountering new people: accustomed to the small groups of hunter-gatherers we almost universally grew up and lived among, the experience of getting to know human beings you hadn't previously encountered would have been relatively rare, and potentially fraught with peril. Members of different tribes might have proven to be out to steal your food supplies and accumulated resources, or even hurt or kill members of your own small group—and they might have covered their intentions with a deceptively welcoming smile.

Today, such conflicts do admittedly still exist, but by the standards of the past they are exceedingly rare, no matter where you live. Few reading this book will ever have been involved in a fight over a piece of food that might mean the difference between life and death; hopefully, fewer still would claim that as a desirable state of humanity to which we should revert. Yet our instincts react as if such conflicts still lie around every corner or behind every smile that greets us—and understanding how deeply untrue that really is might just be your first step toward realigning your personality to a freer, more open, and far healthier attitude toward socialization.

When we tell ourselves we are avoiding social contact in order to protect ourselves, that reasoning is at best only partially true. Underlying that rationalization is not only the instinctive avoidance of confrontation, but also a host of psychological issues that have little to nothing to do with other people. At root, nearly all of these issues boil down to fear: fear of abandonment, fear of disapproval, fear of failure, and perhaps most ironic, fear of loss of social connection. That's right: by triggering our primal fears over being ostracized from the small hunter-gatherer groups we evolved to live among, your fears keep you effectively isolated from the very people who might be able to help relieve those fears. In the long-ago past, the possibility of being ejected from the bosom of one's own tribe would have been a mortal threat, because other groups would have been loath to take on a stranger and the outlook for individual survival was tenuous at best. When you face social rejection, it is such dire circumstances your instincts believe you are risking. But in today's society, where so few people share the level of intimacy necessary to register upon your system as members of your own tribe, people more often isolate themselves by way of removing the possibility for such confrontation, particularly when already suffering from the symptoms of depression.

It is often said, rightfully so, that depression makes everything more difficult. When in the grip of depression, the very notion of sharing your innermost feelings can seem terrifying—but by not doing so, you may inadvertently cut yourself off from the very people who might be best positioned to lessen your suffering. Some severe depression sufferers even come to believe those around them are better off not knowing the truth of their feelings, or that others are better off without them in their lives entirely. In nearly all cases, these types of thoughts are merely rationalizations that enable the processes of social isolation to embed themselves even further, deepening depression and making it significantly more challenging for the sufferer to alleviate their symptoms on their own—yet without the mirror on our own selves that other people can provide, this can become increasingly difficult to recognize.

By maintaining regular contact with friends, family, and other loved ones, especially those who do not suffer from depression or who might suffer less from its symptoms, the depression sufferer can maintain an image of him- or herself other than that which they might construct on their own. Those loved ones might be able to recall a time before the sufferer was enmeshed in depression, a time the sufferer might have forgotten or only dimly remember without prompting. With regular reminders that life was good before depression set in, the depression sufferer can gain renewed hope and vigor in their struggle, bolstering their motivation to maintain anti-depression tactics and habits that can be challenging to keep to alone.

If you have a partner with whom you can enjoy sexual activity, doing so is one of the healthiest things you can do not only for yourself, but for your partner and your relationship with them. As one of the basic human needs, regular sexual contact has been demonstrated to have a positive effect on mood, while the lack of same can deepen depressive spells. Because depression itself can often have libido-decreasing effects, as can some prescription antidepressants, allowing this self-defeating circle to take hold can have devastating effects both on depression sufferers and their partners. If you find yourself trapped in such a cycle, the best thing you can do is discuss your problems with your partner and possibly your doctor: lower dosages or different antidepressants may prove to have fewer undesirable side effects, allowing you to resume a healthy sex life sooner than later.

It should be emphasized that this process of rejuvenated socialization should be recognized for what it is: an ongoing, lifelong practice. Even more than most anti-depression habits, reinvigorating your ability to make social connections is a matter of making many small steps, one at a time over as long as it takes to rebuild a healthy social support structure, whether among friends, family, or both—or best of all, among people who now may be strangers, but might soon be counted as friends. Meditation, guided imagery, hypnotherapy, and mindfulness practices can assist you in reducing anxiety and other symptoms of depression, as well as help you recenter yourself and get in the frame of mind where taking part in social activities is not only conceivable but desirable. Take steps to reduce stress in your life wherever you can, particularly by addressing systematic and recurring stressors and replacing them with healthier, forward-looking alternatives. Consider joining amateur sports leagues, dancing classes, or other activities that combine social contact with exercise. If nothing else, make an effort to do something new each day, and above all, try to have fun. After all, depressed or not, happiness rarely comes to us unbidden like a reward dropping out of the sky; in most cases, you have to go out and find it for yourself.

Once you have begun working to reinvigorate your social connections, do not berate yourself for failing to reestablish the type of close personal friendships you might previously have enjoyed—or perceived other people to enjoy—within a week or two, especially if you have been experiencing the isolating effects of depression for some time. Instead, congratulate yourself for making progress, no matter how small: smiling and greeting a stranger as you pass, making small talk with a cashier or fellow customers during a grocery run, or even chatting with a friend or acquaintance via social media can all represent positive steps forward. Eventually, you will come to recognize these occasions as not highly fraught minefields replete with danger or other anxiety-inducing possibilities, but opportunities to reconnect with humanity, reconstruct your support structure, and assuage your depression along with that of others—for even when you suffer its symptoms personally, depression can be surprisingly difficult to detect in other people. Unfortunately, those selfsame isolating instincts have led many of us to become terribly adept at hiding our interior lives from others, deepening our loneliness even further out of fear of rejection.

When you do connect with another depression sufferer, it can be tempting to make depression itself a recurrent topic of conversation. Yet by doing so, we may inadvertently sabotage our own efforts at reconnection. Depression support groups and other such purpose-oriented organizations aside, defining yourself as 'the person who always brings up depression' in another person's eyes can all too quickly lead them to build a mental association between you and their own depressive tendencies—tendencies they may not wish to be reminded of. Thereby, as that individual makes their own journey forward, through no fault of your own they may come to see you as representative of those depressive symptoms weighing them down, each of your meetings a reminder of how much work they have yet to do.

While you may never experience such circumstances, those who have previously attempted rejuvenation of their social connections will likely find this situation all too familiar. If so, you should not blame yourself; depression can color all aspects of human existence, including friendship, and its pervasive influence can derail many a well-intentioned individual from reaching their goals. Yet it is important to remember that by reestablishing a social support network, you are not directly attempting to lessen your depression so much as mitigate the circumstances which allowed it to take root in the first place, going against the grain of modern culture in a manner that, while entirely natural, others may tend to see as uncharacteristic of you, particularly if you've been suffering from depression for an extended period of time. When you meet such resistance, either from others or from recurrence of your own negative thoughts, challenge them. Rather than letting them dominate you, remember that just as you are not defined by what others perceive you to be, you are also not your thoughts. Both the impressions of others and the thoughts inside your head are only as meaningful or meaningless as you allow them to be, and only you have the ability to choose to what degree you will let them affect you.

It may sound trite, but working towards a positive mindset—that is, simply trying to be happy—can have surprising benefits, especially over the long term. While many of us may instinctively recoil from such a tactic, feeling it to be inherently deceptive, self-deluding, or redolent of well-intentioned advice offered by friends or family who wish you would simply 'snap out' of depression, studies have demonstrated that pretending to be happier can actually have real effects on mood. Yes, simply putting on a happy face alone is unlikely to pull you out of a depression of moderate to major proportions, but it has been shown to encourage social connections, increase encouraging feedback from others, and cause them to be more likely to view you in a positive light. Even patients who have gotten Botox treatment without intention to address symptoms of depression have reported surprisingly consistent positive effects on mood: after the lines etched into their faces were chemically diminished, other people were demonstrated to be less likely to perceive them as frowning all the time, causing them to be perceived as happier people. Thereafter, those people attracted more smiles, gained elevated mood, and enjoyed the benefits of improved social interaction.

While it is unlikely that choosing to seek treatment with Botox or making other cosmetic alterations to your appearance will be the ultimate deciding factor in relieving your depression, other lifestyle changes are significantly easier to implement. Fortunately, as knowledge of depression, isolation, and their corrosive long-term effects continues to spread, not only is the stigma that used to be associated with such conditions less pervasive, but more and more support programs to help people suffering from these conditions are beginning to appear.

However, without your active participation, the existence of such groups isn't enough to change your life. Where defeating depression is concerned, all too often it will fall to you and you alone to make the decisions that will lead you toward a healthier, more fulfilling life. Therefore, is it crucial that you begin taking steps as soon as possible to change isolating habits and emphasize activities that build social connections between you and other people, whether those people be family, current friends, or people you don't know yet. It falls to no one but you to make the effort to not only be more social, but also to recognize opportunities for social contact when they spring up.

Depending on your current state of isolation, chances are good that your instincts in this area might have deteriorated from disuse. This is part of the reason it's good to get into the habit of making small talk with people you encounter as a part of your daily routine: whether or not those people end up becoming close friends or not, each positive interaction not only reinforces your image of yourself as a more social person, but also lubricates your social skills and helps to keep you on top of your game when it matters, minimizing awkward gaps in conversation and other troublesome obstacles. Participation in isolating activities like videogames should be minimized, if not eliminated entirely in favor of more productive leisure time options. If that seems out of reach right now, at the very least try to choose videogames that maximize the illusion of social interaction and acknowledge to yourself that by consciously selecting isolating activities, you may be actively contributing to your own loneliness, or not doing all you can to mitigate it.

In this process of rebuilding your social life, you may find yourself needing to change or even break habits you previously considered intrinsic to your routine. Many of us have rapidly become accustomed to habitually—or even reflexively—glancing at our phones, tablets, or computers every few minutes just in case something happened since the last time they were checked. Consider for a moment: how often would you really have missed anything important by not choosing to look at your device right at any given second? From now on, make the choice to rest assured that had anything worth knowing about happened, you surely would have heard about it later, suffering no loss to yourself, and understand that by devoting your attention to your device, you subtly send the message to everyone around you, whether friend or stranger, that you consider your device eminently more worthy of attention than they are.

Due to the ubiquity of such devices, many people of late have found it beneficial to reduce their levels of engagement and device usage with periodic 'vacations' from either their devices or the social media streams contained therein, thereby limiting their exposure to depressing and triggering stimuli like news (which is so often bad, and so rarely of direct personal import), as well as the stimulating effects of their glowing screens. Others elect to limit their use of electronics after certain times in order to minimize detrimental effects on the quality of their sleep, and still others choose to use time-constraint apps on the devices themselves which limit how, when, and for what purposes the devices can be used. While the jury is still out on the efficacy of such tactics, particularly as used for treatment of depression symptoms, you may well want to consider such a course of action if you begin to notice the familiar tug of addiction where your device is concerned. You might discover that limiting or shortening hours spent engaged with your device produces noticeable benefits in your sense of well-being and connectedness with the world around you, if not better quality sleep and renewed friendships.

Where social media itself and its potential effects upon depression are concerned, at this time the jury is still out. While electronically facilitated social media has been around for decades, it is only recently that it has become a ubiquitous and nearly unavoidable part of our lives. As such, no consensus has been reached on its overall effect on depression. While some lump social media in with all other electronic interactions as a poor substitute for real-life contact, others are cautiously optimistic that social media can produce positive results in strengthening friendships and building new social ties. However, the evidence is beginning to mount: in a recent study of young adults—demographically speaking, the group most likely to use social media regularly—it was found that the more time a subject spent using social media, the more likely they were to be depressed. As we've seen, of course, correlation is not causation, and it could be argued that those suffering from depression were more likely to attempt to placate their symptoms via the electronically facilitated path of least resistance, among other factors. But undoubtedly, these results are cause for concern, at least among those who are attempting to reduce their depression symptoms while heavily engaged with social media. At the very minimum, it might be prudent to take steps to limit use of social media apps to facilitate real-world interactions and to have conversations with people you're acquainted with in real life—not simply to endlessly distract yourself with a continual barrage of items that might or might not be real, but are almost certain to have little to do with improving your symptoms of depression.

Finally, a word regarding toxic people. In the course of alleviating your symptoms of depression, it's possible you may discover that you consistently feel more depressed following interactions with a particular person, who may or may not be depressed themselves. While this person might be a friend, acquaintance, co-worker, or family member, if they are unable or unwilling to curb whatever behaviors exacerbate your depression, or if they prove unsupportive of your efforts to address your depression, it may be difficult to continue that relationship in the same manner as before. Particularly while you are actively ramping up your battle against depression, limiting contact with these individuals is generally the best choice in the short term, depending on their position in your life and the feasibility of doing so. If this is unachievable and you are forced to interact with such a person regularly, keeping the conversation light, brisk, and shallow might be your only option. Once you have had some success controlling your depressive symptoms, you may choose to reengage with such people to whatever degree you feel it healthy—and to the level you feel it productive. If the person in question is a family member, for example, reaching out to them may prove frustrating, but ultimately healing and constructive in the long run; if a co-worker, you may be able to improve your environment and circumstances at your job as well as lowering your ongoing level of stress. But the fact remains that some toxic individuals will inevitably remain stubbornly mired in their unwillingness or inability to change, and there is very little any of us can do to change that. Should this prove to be the case, you may be forced to make the best decision for your own health and either continue limiting your contact with them or even decide to remove them from your life entirely, if practical. If you are speaking with a therapist regularly, you will likely find it productive to discuss these issues with them, but ultimately only you can make the decision whether it is healthy or not to have someone in your life over the long term—and only you bear the responsibility to make choices for the betterment of your health.

CHAPTER 10

FIGHTING DEPRESSION WITH MEDICAL SCIENCE

SOMETIMES, we just can't do everything on our own. When fighting depression, it's important to remember that there is no shame in admitting that you need help. Far too many people suffer needlessly, believing that others will think them weak or unstable for their problems, when in reality depression is one of the most widespread conditions afflicting the modern world. If you have struggled to allay your symptoms of depression in isolation with only limited or no success, it may be time to consult experts in the field who have knowledge beyond the scope of what this slim book can cover. And even if you believe you have previously attempted to reach out to medical professionals about your depression without success, it may be worth trying again—for just as all depressives do not share identical symptoms, different doctors react differently in different circumstances. Furthermore, it is an unavoidable fact that some medical professionals will be more open to courses of treatment that might match up well with your preferences and lifestyle, while others may be limited in their knowledge to a few possible solutions that may or may not serve your purposes. While it might be impossible for all doctors to be thoroughly versed in every potential condition and treatment available, by taking an active interest in your own well-being and discussing what you're doing to remediate your depressive symptoms, your doctor or doctors can gain a better understanding of your condition and the circumstances surrounding it, thereby potentially providing you with more appropriate treatment that may be able to assist you in reaching your goals more quickly than you ever thought possible—but you'll never find out if you don't ask.

Part of the reason many people find medical treatment helpful is that depression can be caused by many, many conditions, some of which a patient might not even be aware he or she is suffering from. Rather than a root cause, your depression might in fact have manifested as a symptom of a completely different physical condition such as thyroid imbalance, or a previously undiagnosed mental health issue such as bipolar disorder. In many cases, only a trained medical professional will have the expertise to recognize and diagnose these circumstances, either through blood screening, CT or MRI scans, electroencephalograms or other means. By catching such problems early, you stand a better chance of making a complete recovery, and if it is determined you do not suffer from any such illnesses, you have still made progress toward defeating your depression by eliminating potential contributing factors, getting both you and your doctor closer to the root causes of your condition.

Unfortunately, due to many reasons, many people have an ingrained mistrust of or other unhealthy relationship to the medical profession. Yet, many of these selfsame individuals make the mistake of believing that they can diagnose their own symptoms, prescribe an effective remedy, and correct whatever ails them with a few simple keystrokes on an internet resource like WebMD. Other recall their own past frustrations communicating their issues to general practitioners who might have been ill-equipped to treat emotional disorders, or who might have been brought up and trained in a time when conditions such as depression and anxiety were not recognized as the widespread problems we now know them to be. Still others place all responsibility for their health upon their doctors and the treatment they provide without recognizing their own role in maintaining their well-being and end up disappointed that medical treatment failed to correct all of their ills. Rarely are any of these attitudes healthy or productive, though it is understandable how many people come to arrive at such outlooks through years of repeated rationalizations or misunderstandings.

Another widespread misconception about mental health treatment is that medical doctors can only dispense prescription medication and will do little else to address such issues as depression; people who hold this opinion may refer to such doctors derisively as 'pill-pushers' or believe them to be pawns of the drug companies. In fact, medical science recognizes the efficacy of a range of treatments for depression, which may or may not be recommended based upon the severity of your depressive symptoms, and many doctors reserve antidepressant medication for treatment of moderate to severe cases of depression. Furthermore, many doctors will enthusiastically recommend many of the options for relieving depression symptoms covered in this book, only for their advice to fall upon deaf ears as their patient fixates only on the prescription they have convinced themselves will solve their problems without any additional effort on their part—mistakenly, in most cases where depression is concerned.

Whatever your personal opinion of the medical profession, one thing should be emphasized: if you choose to consult a doctor regarding your symptoms of depression, that action alone does not absolve you from working towards reducing your depression, regardless of whether or not that doctor ends up prescribing antidepressant medication to you or not. As discussed earlier, most antidepressant drugs have relatively low success rates, but a large part of the reason for that is that many patients expect the drugs to do the work for them, rather than using them as part of an overall program to control their depression. Throughout the course of this book, we have seen how a wide range of factors can contribute to depression, including emotional, physical, environmental, historical, evolutionary, and chemical, among others. At best, even the most effective and appropriate prescription antidepressant can only remediate those factors directly related to the brain's chemistry and how it affects mood. But particularly if your condition is severe, consultation with a trained medical professional—such as a psychiatrist who diligently keeps abreast of the most recent developments in the field—may well be your best option for finding a course of action to lead you out of depression.

That said, the landscape of medical science is changing constantly, with new treatments, medications, and tactics arising all the time, especially in the field of mental health. Additionally, while taking in this information from the position of a depressed person seeking potential treatment, it can be all too easy to fixate upon scary-sounding worst-case scenario side effects and mentally associate them with a particular treatment—an unproductive approach, at best, and at worst a good way to attach unnecessary free-floating anxiety to medical procedures that you will most likely never undergo. In any case, whatever your current condition it is advisable to investigate any and all solutions offered through your insurance or wellness programs available to you in order to find the doctor or course of action that is most appropriate to remedy your suffering.

With that in mind, this book will not attempt to deliver a comprehensive examination of every treatment currently available, as to attempt to do so would only serve to make it immediately out of date as well as do a disservice to the depth and intricacy of study required of medical professionals. Instead, we will present a brief overview of some of the options you might be presented with during medical treatment for depression, prefaced with the caveat that while you may well elect to be as informed as possible regarding the range of available treatments for depression, chances are slim you will need to know much more than the basic outline of a procedure unless a medical professional recommends a particular course of action in your case.

Psychotherapy, frequently called talk therapy or more generally, counseling, is perhaps the least intrusive method of treating depression and is often considered as a first line of defense against mild to moderate cases. Used alone, psychotherapy is likely to be insufficient against severe depression, but is regularly recommended as part of a comprehensive program of treatment. Benefits of psychotherapy generally include reduced stress levels, increased skills and abilities to cope with problems, heightened understanding of the causes of one's individual depressive disorder, and the perspective to identify habits and behaviors that may worsen depression. There are many kinds of psychotherapy sessions, including individual one-on-one therapy and group therapy, some of which can include spouses or other family members, and many different types of therapy as well: cognitive behavioral therapy is generally centered on getting the depression sufferer to recognize how their own actions, behavior, and thoughts may contribute to their condition, while interpersonal therapy concentrates upon one's relationships with other people. Not all psychiatrists, psychoanalysts, or therapists offer all types of therapy, and not all types of therapy are appropriate for all patients; consult your doctor to find a course of treatment that fits for you. And if you find a certain therapist or course of treatment fails to elicit the desired results, don't be afraid to go back and try again, either with a different therapist or type of therapy.

As you likely know by now, prescription antidepressants are medicines administered under the direction of a doctor or other medical professional which are intended to remediate the symptoms of moderate to major depression. While most readers of this book will be familiar with at least a few such heavily-advertised medications, the number and range of antidepressants offered by drug manufacturers may surprise you: as awareness of the widespread nature of depression and its rapid rise to prominence has spread, so has the realization that this massive population of depressed individuals constitutes a substantial market for products intended to remedy the condition. Additionally, because no prescription antidepressant has yet been demonstrated to significantly lessen depression symptoms in a majority of patients, the market continues to see ongoing research and development of new medications and treatments, and will likely do so for some time.

As noted, prescription antidepressants have been shown to be more effective at mitigating the symptoms of depression when used as part of an overall program for addressing the condition. If you have been prescribed any of the below antidepressants—or others not yet on the market at the time of this book's publication—always be certain to follow your doctor's advice regarding frequency and amount of dosage. Most prescription antidepressants require a significant amount to time to accumulate sufficiently in the body to produce effective results—generally ranging from two to eight weeks—and maintaining the dosage levels recommended by your doctor is crucial to most antidepressants' effectiveness. Make sure to let your doctor know about any other activities you are undertaking to address your depression as well, particularly as regards food, exercise, and any substances or medications you are taking (whether to address your depression or for other reasons) which might interact with your antidepressant medication. And whether or not you find the medication prescribed for you to be effective at remediating your symptoms, never stop taking antidepressants all at once or 'cold turkey' without consulting your doctor. By doing so, you could place yourself at risk for antidepressant discontinuation syndrome or withdrawal. While most antidepressant medications are not conventionally habit-forming or addictive, because antidepressants function by affecting levels of neurotransmitters and other substances in the brain, sudden changes can produce a range of potentially problematic physiological and psychological effects including nausea, insomnia, flu-like symptoms, fatigue, headache, and vomiting. If you are considering stopping any prescription antidepressant therapy, consult your doctor for the best way to ease yourself off the drug and immediately report any negative side effects you experience; your doctor may be able to suggest or prescribe medicines to reduce or eliminate your discontinuation symptoms.

Selective serotonin reuptake inhibitors, or SSRIs, are currently the most widely prescribed type of antidepressant medication, and function primarily by affecting the brain's ability to process serotonin. Brand names for SSRI antidepressants include many you are probably familiar with: Prozac, Paxil, Zoloft, Lexapro, Celexa, and Luvox. Side effects of SSRI medications can include nausea, dizziness, insomnia, fatigue, and sexual side effects including loss of libido and difficulty achieving orgasm.

Serotonin and norepinephrine reuptake inhibitors, or SNRIs, work much like SSRIs but also affect the brain's use of norepinephrine, along with serotonin. Brand names for SNRI antidepressants include Effexor, Pristiq, Cymbalta, and Fetzima; most common side effects reported from SNRI use are similar to those of SSRIs.

Monoamine oxidase inhibitors, or MAOIs, are an older type of antidepressant drugs that have largely been phased out in favor of SSRIs and SNRIs, but are still occasionally prescribed, primarily in situations when a patient has not responded favorably to other types of drugs. MAOIs can produce potentially dangerous interactions with a number of other medications including painkillers, cough syrups, and decongestants; for these reasons, patients taking MAOIs must also avoid certain foods such as aged meats and cheeses. Brand names for MAOI antidepressants include Parnate, Nardil, Marplan, and Emsam.

Similarly, tricyclic antidepressants, or TCAs, are also an older category of antidepressants that tend not to be prescribed often due to undesirable side effects, including stomach upset, blood pressure and blood sugar level changes, dry mouth, and dizziness. Brand names for TCAs include Norpramin, Elavil, Vivactil, and Pamelor.

Other antidepressant medications that do not fall into any of the above categories include bupropion, sold under the brand name Wellbutrin; trazodone, sold as Desyrel; and mirtazapine, marketed as Remeron, each of which carries its own potential side effects. No matter which antidepressant your doctor recommends for you, be sure to keep in touch regarding the medication's efficacy in reducing your symptoms of depression and inform him or her about any disagreeable side effects you might experience. In certain circumstances when a patient does not obtain the desired effect from a particular drug, a second medication such as a stimulant or anti-anxiety medication may be prescribed to boost the antidepressant's effects or to address undesirable side effects. Additionally, because different people respond differently to different medications, finding the best antidepressant for a given situation can be a matter of trial and error in certain patients; if you do not experience any significant reduction in your depression symptoms following the period delineated by your doctor, you may need to be switched to a different medication.

Beyond therapy and prescription antidepressants, a wide range of depression treatments exists to address a number of differing conditions and types of depression. Hormone replacement therapy, or HRT, is specifically used for treating certain types of depression that appear in people whose bodies are not delivering the same amounts of hormones such as estrogen and testosterone to their system as they once did. While HRT is most commonly used to treat depression in women undergoing menopause, the therapy is also used to treat men with low levels of testosterone and has proven quite effective at lessening depression symptoms in both women and men. However, because HRT is a treatment designed only to address the specific problem of changing or fluctuating hormone levels, it is not to be considered for those suffering more general depression symptoms unconnected to hormonal changes.

Electroconvulsive therapy or ECT, popularly known as electric shock therapy, consists of applying electrical stimulation to the brain while a patient rests under general anesthesia. ECT is generally reserved for cases in which prescribed antidepressants and other courses of action have failed to significantly relieve severe depression. While many people may be familiar with ECT from popular depictions of the therapy from old movies, the treatment has been considerably refined and improved to target more specific regions of the brain, using less current than in the past. Though many people hold preconceptions about this type of treatment, in practice it has proven among the safest and most effective: ECT is painless, and generally produces results much more quickly than antidepressant medications, making it an optimal choice for those suffering from extremely severe cases of depression. ECT has proven fairly potent at alleviating the symptoms of sufferers of treatment-resistant depression, producing positive results in over two-thirds of treatment-resistant patients after two to three weeks—twice the success rate of antidepressants—though the number of ECT sessions can vary depending on the specifics of an individual's needs. The most common side effect of ECT treatment is short-term memory loss or brief confusion following treatment along with occasional physical effects such as headaches, nausea, or muscle pain.

Transcranial magnetic stimulation, or TMS, consists of an electromagnetic coil placed alongside the head, which creates a magnetic field that produces an electric current, stimulating nerve cells in the prefrontal cortex to improve mood. TMS is the least invasive of the direct brain stimulation treatments, and like ECT is most often recommended for patients with treatment-resistant depression who have not experienced improvement of their symptoms after taking prescription antidepressants. Because TMS is less powerful than ECT, the patient does not need to be placed under sedation during treatment; however, TMS is also not as effective as ECT at alleviating symptoms of severe depression, and cannot be used on patients with pacemakers.

Vagus nerve stimulation, or VNS, is a newer technique that involves implanting a small device under the skin which delivers direct stimulation to the vagus nerve via electrical pulses to help control mood. Similarly, deep brain stimulation, or DBS, involves surgically implanting a pair of electrodes into a patient's brain, using a pulse generator implanted in the patient's chest to send impulses to the implanted electrodes. Currently both VNA and DBS are rarely used and generally reserved for extreme cases in which a sufferer of treatment-resistant severe depression has been shown to be unable to be helped through other treatments. As these treatments are studied further, more will undoubtedly be learned regarding their safety and effectiveness, as well as the long-term outlook for treatment-resistant depression sufferers treated with VNS or DBS.

Finally, a treatment for depression that has been used for centuries but is only now becoming widely accepted and studied is marijuana, or cannabis. Recent studies have indicated marijuana may be highly effective at treating some forms of depression, particularly when chronic stress is a contributing factor, and that regular marijuana use may produce elevated serotonin levels without the negative side effects associated with SSRIs and other prescription antidepressants. Other research has indicated that heavy marijuana smokers may be more likely to be depressed, though no causal relationship between marijuana use and increased depression symptoms has been shown to exist, suggesting that heavy marijuana smokers may largely be attempting to self-medicate in order to reduce their depression symptoms. As marijuana continues to achieve legalization and acceptance throughout wide ranges of the United States and much of the social stigma previously associated with it vanishes, many people from all walks of life have reported success addressing their depression symptoms with marijuana use. However, because most research is just now only in its early stages, few guidelines for dosage, frequency, or strains of marijuana that might best address depression symptoms currently exist. If you live in an area where marijuana is an option and you choose to attempt remediation of your depression symptoms with marijuana, begin with small doses, use the marijuana in the safest way possible—edibles are generally considered the delivery method with the least impact on the body, followed by vaporization, with smoking as the least desirable delivery system for medical purposes—and choose strains containing high percentages of cannabidiol, or CBD, a cannabinoid that has been shown to produce therapeutic effects without the psychoactive effects of high-THC strains. If in doubt whether treatment with marijuana might be right for you, particularly if you are currently being treated with prescription antidepressants or other medical treatment, consult your doctor before attempting to address your depression symptoms with marijuana.

CHAPTER 11

PUTTING IT ALL TOGETHER AND STAYING DEPRESSION-FREE FOR LIFE

AS you likely know all too well, even when depression has been defeated once, the condition is likely to recur. Most depression sufferers will experience four to five episodes during the course of their lives, but others may experience more, particularly as statistics regarding the spread of depression continue to rise. Sometimes this may be due to internal biology or unaddressed lifestyle issues such as an ongoing lack of exercise, but life changes can trigger the onset of an episode of depression in many people, especially those with a prior history of depression.

Unfortunately, depressive tendencies often increase with age, along with the frequency of occurrence of potentially depression-triggering incidents. Because there is little any of us can do to change either of these facts, it is of paramount importance that we develop strong depression-coping skills as early in life as possible so that they become ingrained, familiar habits we can rely upon when needed. If life were fair, by the time any of us would be called upon to deal with major life events we would have fully-developed coping mechanisms in place to help us get through difficult times—but as you no doubt realize by now, more often than not things don't work that way.

From the perspective of youth, it is easy to surmise that those of more advanced ages would have gained wisdom enough to make handling life's slings and arrows more feasible, but as people age, distressingly often a cumulative lack of stress handling faculties can build into a deeply-rooted antipathy to new solutions, even when they may offer the promise of renewed enjoyment of life. In truth, study after study has demonstrated that one's outlook on life can have tangible, lasting effects well outside the boundaries of one's own mind: negative viewpoints translate to negative effects both upon mood and physiology—and perhaps even more alarming, on lifespan. One long-term study of Ohio residents demonstrated positive outlook on life translated to an average seven and a half year increase in life expectancy, an increase equal to the decrease inflicted by such still-insoluble diseases such as diabetes or cancer.

When viewed in this light, the severity of the impact of depression should be starkly clear: if its effects can lead to a decrease in lifespan equal to that of some of humanity's most feared diseases, depression should never be minimized as 'merely' a personality disorder. Depression has tangible, life-eroding effects that can not only shorten life but also decrease one's ability to enjoy it, the same as any other disease. Unfortunately, negative thoughts don't come with glaring messages printed on them the way cigarettes do, but perhaps we would do well to condition ourselves as if they did: "just one won't hurt," we tell ourselves when indulging our weakness for fatalistic thoughts, and perhaps just one occurrence might not—but once it becomes a persistent habit, chances are slight that we'll still escape unscathed.

By learning to resist our negative, depressive thoughts and understanding the risks we take by allowing ourselves to wallow in unproductive rumination on such thoughts, we can bolster our resistance to depression and train ourselves to minimize the effects of depression on our lives. We may never be able to banish the specter of depression entirely; once a person has felt the touch of depression, they are more likely to experience it again than someone who has never suffered a depressive spell. But by developing ingrained, tried and tested defenses against depression's effects, we can proceed with confidence, knowing that having beaten depression once, we can do it again—and thus, break its terrifying hold on us for good.

Some people have a tendency to become entranced by the 'glamor' of depression, causing them to cling to their condition and harmful habits linked to it out of a mistaken belief that it somehow sets them apart or makes them special. Trapped in the throes of depression, they may see people they believe to be happy and reject their company, thinking them shallow and incapable of understanding them. In truth, this type of self-elevating thinking is self-defeating, leading inevitably to isolation, loneliness, and depression—and ironically, those figures such a type may think of as blithely happy are just as likely to be concealing their own depression or other emotional issues.

Thanks to the lack of perspective the mirror provides, these tendencies can be difficult to recognize in ourselves. However, I suspect most will be able to point to one or more negatively-inclined individuals they have encountered in the past whose poor outlook and consistently unpleasant demeanor ended up affecting their lives for the worse. The problem with this type of thinking, of course, is that as we've seen, depression is neither rare nor special in any way. Depression affects people of all races, genders, and economic means, and should not be seen as either a badge of honor or a mark of superiority. Bearing the brand of depression is no indication of uniqueness; rather, it is simply an illness requiring treatment, no more or less special than any other.

Occasionally, depression has been linked to creativity, though not in any legitimate or clinical manner, and usually not by those actually suffering from the condition. Sadness can play its part in inspiring artistic creation, of course, and even if tearjerkers aren't one's genre of choice, sad occurrences are often necessary for the creation of dramatic tension in both fiction and nonfiction—it's difficult to imagine many of Shakespeare's plays without them. But most often, those who truly suffer from ongoing depression report inability to engage with their creative abilities while in the grip of a depressive spell, only managing to reengage with their creative powers once they've succeeded in crawling out of the depths of depression. Ironically, the process of artistic creation itself can be an effective treatment for depression, helping to ameliorate depressive symptoms whether that creativity takes the form of writing, drawing, painting, playing music, or any other form of creative effort. If you have a creative hobby you enjoy, you should try to set time aside to indulge your creative side on a regular basis, particularly when you feel the tendrils of depression beginning to take root. You do not have to address depression as a topic of your creative efforts in any way to gain the benefits of creative work, but if you do choose to engage with your depressive tendencies through your creativity you might well find your subconscious mind working through your problems with an uncharacteristic rapidity. Naturally, some opt to maintain their creative endeavors as a respite from the stresses of reality, and there is also value in this approach: the experience of returning to a long-simmering creative project can often feel like a comfortable refuge from problems that can seem inescapable, whether depression or otherwise. The great thing about individual creative work is that it's entirely up to you which approach to take, and no matter which you decide you will benefit regardless.

Notwithstanding your position in life, take comfort that seeking treatment for your depression will not make you any less special or unique than having a wart or callus removed from your foot—or perhaps more apt, taking antibiotics to treat an infection, which if left untreated might grow over time to become a life-threatening condition. The analogy of diabetes is often used to characterize the ongoing management of depression symptoms over the course of a lifetime: like diabetes, you may not be able to eradicate the condition entirely, but with help you can learn to manage its symptoms when necessary. By doing so, you stand the best chance of enjoying a long, healthy, and rewarding life with as little recurrence of depression as possible.

AFTERWORD

Now that you've learned a number of strategies for beating your depression, I encourage you to put these plans into action as soon as you can—immediately, if possible—and even when you don't feel as if you're making any progress, don't give up. Within as short a time as a few days to a week, by making small changes in your daily routine and choices you can achieve startling reductions in your depressive symptoms. And when you do, don't stop! It is all too easy to lapse back into the path of least resistance, thus undoing all the good work we might have accomplished, and I can assure you from experience that it is much easier to keep going than it is to get started in the first place.

This book has deliberately been designed to be relatively brief; as such, you should revisit it as often as you feel necessary to reinforce the positive habits you are working to create. If you're not ready to get started, I understand and sympathize. Fighting depression takes time and energy, and many people suffering from depression may feel as if they have precious little of either. Yet by taking even very small steps forward, you may be surprised at the effects you are able to produce in yourself. The most important principle to remember is that when it comes to fighting depression, doing something, no matter how seemingly insignificant, is always better than doing nothing. Before you know it, small steps can add up to big progress, and the unthinkably huge obstacle your depression once seemed will be reduced to much more manageable levels.

Finally, I would like to leave you with this: above all, be kind to yourself, both in thought and action. Because the truth is, everyone deserves to live the kind of life that is possible with the knowledge that depression can absolutely be controlled—and my deepest wish is for you and the rest of humanity to achieve that state, one way or another, once and for all.

Until we meet again: be well, and stay well.

THE END